Stop Being Shy

A Guide on How to Talk to Anyone

Monica Lynn

Table of Contents

Introduction

Do you have an interesting and fulfilling life that only exists in your head? Do you see yourself as engaging and interesting but are too shy to let others see the amazing person you are? Are you craving human interaction but are afraid you will be judged for seeking it? According to research, 60% of people in Eastern cultures and 40% of those in Western cultures are afflicted by shyness (Carducci, 2017). This means that you are not alone. Millions of people suffer from shyness and even more were able to get through it. You too can be like those who shed their timid nature and went on to feel more comfortable in social interactions. You might be wondering how I know? Well, I used to be shy too and I worked hard to find a way to overcome my shyness and make the most of my life.

Like you, I used to have difficulty socializing and connecting with new people due to my shyness. I would often feel self-conscious, wondering if people are talking behind my back or judging me—and I know that you feel the same way. You are probably tired of the missed opportunities and experiences that pass you by because you're too shy to say yes and step out of your comfort zone. I also know that you are desperate to reach out and form connections with others, but you find it challenging to maintain friendships or thrive in social situations. Being shy also means you find it hard to express your thoughts and opinions to large groups of people, which may make you seem disinterested in what's going on around you. This can lead to feeling lonely and isolated from your peers, which is something that you might be dealing with right now.

Shyness can negatively affect your social skills and behavior which will lead to you not being able to integrate well with your peer group. Being shy makes it harder to be included and accepted. It's unfortunate that shyness can lead to people having negative opinions about you such as you are less intelligent and not having anything meaningful to contribute to discussions and debates, which is absolutely not true. According to Ekua & Quansah, "When it comes to examining how shyness affects the interaction with people, it was found that there was a negative relationship" (2016, p. 24). Children who are considered shy have a hard time communicating with their age mates and will often prefer to play by themselves so that they do not get caught up in any embarrassing scenarios. Furthermore, studies show that they will inevitably receive treatment from their peers due to their shyness (Ekua & Quansah, 2016).

Your shyness could stem from overthinking. Every moment you are awake, your mind is thinking about various things in order to make decisions, reflect, or analyze certain aspects of your life. A problem arises when you cannot control the way you think and your mental activity morphs into overthinking, which then suffocates and exhausts you. Overthinking produces unproductive emotions and thought patterns which can cause you to become shy. When your mind is in a negative mental loop it can lead to rumination which will disrupt your daily activities and throw off your mood and emotions. Overthinking situations might make you shy away from making connections with others and building relationships. This will increase your anxiety and social situations causing you mental stress and unnecessary obsessing on what you did right or wrong. The act of overthinking may make you more shy, exacerbate irritability, insomnia, and increase tension in your neck and shoulders.

If you have been struggling with shyness and forming connections with others then *Stop Being Shy* is the right book for you. By reading this book and implementing its tips and strategies you will be better equipped to identify your triggers and negative patterns. I will also share with you how to learn the skill of empowering self-talk and utilizing affirmations to build your self-confidence. It is important to understand that this book will push you out of your comfort zone. Overcoming your shyness using the techniques offered in this book may make you feel uncomfortable at first, but if you learn how to be mindful and self-aware you will realize that it is for your benefit. As you read through the chapters, they will also teach you how to cope with your social anxiety so that you can learn how to network and establish mutually beneficial professional relationships. Furthermore, this book will teach you how to socialize in the rapidly evolving technological world of today. In the end you will also learn how to remain assertive while maintaining your boundaries and accepting your vulnerability and authenticity that stems from your shyness.

I am passionate about helping you overcome your shyness because it has held me back in my life. I watched my friends and family advance in their personal lives and their careers because I avoided situations that terrified me. Even if I did tell myself that I would do something, my shyness would change my mind at the last minute. My quality of life was not where I wanted to be and no matter where I looked, I could not find resources or self-help books that spoke about overcoming shyness. Once I decided that I was going to get over being timid I then developed certain skills that I still use today. These are the skills that I want to pass on to you through this book. I know exactly how you are feeling and where you are emotionally. Luckily, your life is about to take a different direction if you learn to implement the things I talk about in this book. Because I have walked in your shoes, I have taken the initiative to be your guide through this journey. You can overcome your shyness and I'm here to show you how. No one was there to hold my hand, but I am here to hold yours.

From today onward, you no longer have to walk in a room and feel awkward or tense. After learning all the techniques and methods I used to overcome my own shyness, you will also learn how to minimize the symptoms of shyness like profusely sweating, having an upset stomach or an excessively high heart rate. You are no longer a prisoner of your timidness because I am officially setting you free. While your shyness won't be automatically conquered, you should feel assured that you are taking steps in the right direction to reclaim your confidence. Because you have picked up this book, you have made significant progress as you acknowledge that your shyness is inhibiting your life. The first step is identifying the problem and acknowledging its existence in your life, and you have done that, well done! The next steps are yet to come, and you will discover them as the chapters of this book unfold. Always remember to be patient and kind to yourself throughout this journey because you are doing your best and that on its own is commendable. So many people turn away from their social awkwardness, but you have decided to face it and overcome it, come what may.

Imagine walking into a room with your head held high and your shoulder squared with all the confidence in the world. Imagine looking everybody in the eye and smiling as you offer greetings to the group. Can you see yourself flourish in that situation as you make a conversation with anybody who wishes to speak to you? Can you picture yourself laughing and taking the contacts of the new people that you have connected with? If you can't yet picture it in your mind, I implore you to let your imagination run wild. Take the time to visualize yourself being a hit every time you walk into a room. Picture yourself maintaining eye contact with somebody you are having an engaging conversation with. Envision yourself having lengthy chats with different individuals at a party or social gathering. Insert yourself in this new life because it is yours to claim now! That life is within reach. After reading this book you will shed your old life of shyness and step into a confident and assertive personality that seizes every opportunity to be successful. Are you ready to stop being a shy pebble and become a little boulder? Shake up that nervous system because it is now time to *Stop Being Shy*!

Chapter 1:

Identifying Triggers and

Patterns

Have you ever wondered why you are shy in the first place? Is there something that happened that caused you to be this way or were you born like this? It is normal to wonder and ask questions especially when your shyness is making your life difficult. To tackle shyness and what triggers it, it is important to first unpack what shyness is so that you can understand its patterns. Shyness is considered a reaction to feeling fear when you get into a social situation where someone is trying to speak to you, or you have to approach another person. Being shy is characterized as that feeling of hesitation, nervousness or agitation when confronted with the potential of interaction with others. The Merriam-Webster dictionary defines shy as "easily frightened: timid; disposed to avoid a person or thing; sensitively diffident or retiring: reserved." There are numerous things that contribute to shyness such as how you were parented, or the things that you experienced in your life. This chapter will be focusing on exploring what triggers your shyness and how to rise up against those shy-inducing scenarios and patterns.

Recognizing Specific Situations or Triggers That Exacerbate Shyness

A trigger is something that can evoke an extreme reaction to a situation. It is an extremely emotional response to a situation that makes you feel similar to how you felt in a negative situation from the past. The various triggers that evoke your shyness will differ from the next person's triggers. Their shyness might emanate from the way that they were raised whilst yours may stem from a traumatic past experience. In order to truly understand what triggers your shyness you need to explore where your shyness stems from. There are a few qualities that can cause you to feel shy including a lack of self-esteem, being self-conscious, being afraid of what people will say about you, and fear of being rejected. Feeling shy is evitable if you think that people have nothing good to say about you or if you are constantly comparing yourself to somebody who has a more outspoken or colorful personality and is well liked among your peers. Feeling these kinds of feelings about yourself can lead to you shying away from social situations but there are also other triggers that can cause you to withdraw into yourself.

Although your triggers can be unique, there are common situations that can lead to shyness that are experienced by a majority of the public. Going on a date or meeting new people can cause you to feel shy. Standing in front of a large crowd and making a speech or any kind of public speaking can also make you want to run for cover. Other shy-inducing activities include speaking in a meeting or being called on during class to answer a question or give your opinion. You might just be one of those people that cannot cope with being the center of attention or having to be observed while you do something. These triggers might not only make you shy but also a number of other people around you. It might be comforting to know that even great people throughout history suffered from shyness when they came into these situations. Abraham Lincoln, Rosa Parks as well as Steven Spielberg have been described as soft-spoken and reserved and yet they were able to achieve so much despite being shy.

Your body can have a variety of reactions to your triggers such as physical, emotional and cognitive reactions. Having these responses point to something being a trigger, so it is important to pay attention to how you feel in any given situation so that you can try to identify what your triggers are. Firstly, physical responses include:

- having tense shoulders or neck

- experiencing a knot in your stomach

- experiencing what feels like a racing heart or palpitations

- profuse sweating

Secondly, emotional responses could manifest as any of the following:

- feeling very panicked

- feeling extremely nervous

- feeling trapped in the situation

- feeling fearful

Lastly, cognitive reactions to your triggers include:

- fearing that you will be rejected

- experiencing heightened self-consciousness

- thinking that nobody cares or needs you

- fearing disapproval

- fearing exclusion

Once you have identified what your shyness triggers are, you can start to work toward being aware of when they occur and controlling how you react in those situations.

Uncovering Patterns and Common Themes in Shyness-Inducing Scenarios

Identifying what your triggers are means evaluating how you react to certain situations. Identifying triggers involves analyzing situations of the past that evoked an intense and unjustified reaction. Are there any similar situations in your past? What was the topic that was being discussed or the event that was taking place? Try to compartmentalize the various sections of the discussion or the event and notice where your emotions changed. Isolating the different parts of what occurred will show you the exact moment that triggered you. Was it something someone said about you that triggered emotions from the past rooted in your childhood or did a thought enter into your mind that reinforces negative beliefs about yourself. Getting down to exactly what your triggers are it's not an easy process and it can get quite uncomfortable when you face reality and elements of your past. Take your time to analyze every situation where you feel shy and unpack it. Get as detailed as you can and use a journal to write it all down so that you can review your analysis whenever a similar situation comes into play.

You may realize that you are stuck in a pattern of behavior where you are triggered by certain situations and react in the same way over and over again. Try to isolate the thoughts that run through your mind when you experience shyness coupled with the emotions you feel. The feelings and thoughts that you experience right before getting shy are the precursors that can help you take control in the moment. It is important to be aware of how you feel while you are triggered as it points to a certain pain that you may be experiencing or dealing with. Acknowledging your feelings is important as they paint a picture of how you feel in the present; being aware of your emotions and mental states give you an opportunity to assess the reason why you feel that way so that you're not delaying dealing with any issues in your life. Remember not to attach your identity to your feelings as "I am sad", "I am angry" but try to say, "I am feeling sad" or "I am feeling angry". It is normal to be afraid of judgment from those around you. Nobody wants to be rejected or feel as if they are not good enough and these are common fears in everyone. Just because something is common does not make it true.

Strategies for Managing and Overcoming Specific Triggers

In a perfect world you would be able to avoid your triggers completely but that is not realistic. You will be triggered, and you may even feel shy on a daily basis. This might make you feel as if you are not in control. You will feel more empowered once you know what your triggers are as you develop a personalized toolkit to manage them. If you're afraid of public speaking but have to frequently address people, then you could try to meditate and do some affirmations before you speak and write down your speaking points on cue cards. Whatever it is that calms you down, you should incorporate it into your trigger management process. Feelings of anxiety will take you right before you start to feel shy so it can also be beneficial to learn a few relaxation techniques. Deep breathing exercises are an example of a relaxation technique that you could utilize when you are triggered and feel as if you are going to succumb to your shyness.

To manage the effect of your triggers, you can also develop relaxing habits that ease your mental state and help to alleviate your anxiety. One such habit is deep breathing. When you are feeling stressed, the way you breathe is altered which is known to prolong anxious feelings (Department of Health & Human Services, 2015). By learning how to control your breathing when you are shy or stressed, you can improve the symptoms you experience in those scenarios. Some benefits of deep breathing include (Department of Health & Human Services, 2015):

- feeling more vitalized and refreshed

- better immune response

- more normalized heart rate and blood pressure

- less stress hormone (cortisol) in the blood

- an improved balance of carbon dioxide and oxygen in the blood

As a start you can practice the following deep breathing technique: inhale through your nose using your diaphragm for four seconds; hold your breath for a further four seconds and exhale forcefully through your mouth for eight seconds. Repeat this until you feel relaxed.

Another relaxation technique you could use to ease your mind and anxiety is mindfulness. Being mindful is a helpful way to allow you to cope with life as it unfolds in real time. According to Sutton, "Mindfulness has the potential to switch off or manage emotional reactivity to anxiety-inducing situations; it helps people pause, rise above the turmoil, see with greater clarity, and respond with freedom" (2022, para. 12). There are various mindful techniques you can use such as taking a mindful pause when you feel triggered or removing yourself from the situation and observing from the outside as an objective party. Both these exercises mean that you are no longer having an automatic reaction to a scenario that is emotionally triggering. The more you practice these relaxation techniques, the less apprehensive you will become when you are put in situations that trigger you. In the end, you will build resilience toward your triggers.

Developing Resilience in the Face of Challenging Situations

Consider yourself an observer in your life. Watch and acknowledge all the good and all the bad that happens in you. Take note of the way you react and why you react in that way. You will soon start to see that there is so much good in your life, and the things that happen are not personal. The world is not out to get you. Changing your perspective on life and developing an objective view on all the things that occur in your daily life will allow you to build emotional resilience. Having a good attitude about where you are and where you are going will also allow you the grace to appreciate the journey you are on. Being overly critical of yourself and the mistakes you have made will add strain to your mental well-being so congratulate yourself on things you did right in your life and encourage yourself to try again with the things you have failed at. A positive mindset and self-talk will help to improve how to cope with stressful situations when they occur.

The bad things that you think are going to happen when you're afraid to do something are almost always far worse than what would actually happen. Instead of caving into the negative thoughts or trauma that led you to be shy, you can choose to face your fear and do the thing that you are shying away from. For example, if you are afraid of standing up and contributing to a meeting in front of your colleagues, you could choose to take a small stand against your shyness and say some closing remarks at the end of the meeting. Try not to succumb to your fear but rather challenge those feelings by telling yourself that they stem from a place of insecurity and untruths. By choosing to stand against your shyness you will develop resilience every time you feel afraid and uncertain. Confident people feel exactly how you feel. The only difference between them and you are that they choose to face their fears every time instead of shying away from them. You can be like that too; it just takes a bit of practice.

The information I have shared with you in this chapter will empower you not only to face and identify your triggers and patterns, but to also understand their root cause. You now have a deeper understanding of what triggers your shyness. From here you are able to face it head on and overcome the triggers that have been holding you back. The following chapter will explore how to reform your self-talk by using positive affirmations. You are well on your way to a new and awesome life, just keep reading.

Chapter 2:

Empowering Self-Talk and

Affirmations

Have you ever taken the time to listen to your inner voice? When you are doing something and things go wrong, do you encourage yourself to try again or are you admonishing yourself? There is a constant inner dialogue that goes on in your mind and depending on whether it is positive or negative, it can either help to reduce or increase your shyness. By exploring how to harness the power of self-talk and using affirmations to increase your confidence, you can learn how to develop a powerful inner dialogue and eventually overcome your shyness. Along with identifying triggers you can use positive self-talk and affirmations as tools to reduce the inhibiting effects of shyness. This chapter will teach you how to shift your mindset and adopt positive thinking habits and develop an optimistic inner dialogue.

Harnessing the Power of Positive Self-Talk to Overcome Shyness

Having positive thoughts can often improve your stress levels when life is just not going your way. Someone who is pessimistic may blame themselves when things go wrong even when it's out of their control. An optimistic person knows that there are a lot of outside forces that come into play when things go wrong. Whether you have positive or negative thoughts will influence and have a great impact on the kind of self-talk you partake in. When you have positive thinking patterns it doesn't mean that you are simply ignoring all the bad things that are happening in your life. Positive thoughts often emanate from positive self-talk that can either come from your conscious thoughts, logical reasoning, misconceptions or preconceived ideas. Self-talk reflects how you see things in the world. It is usually shaped by your childhood and the things that you experienced; sometimes your self-talk is even shaped by the positive or negative things you were told repeatedly by your parents. In the end, your self-talk will be the backbone of how you handle your thoughts and emotions.

Due to the fact that self-talk is a reflection of your inner voice it can heavily influence how stressed you feel. Negative self-talk can make your life more stressful as it adds anxiety and reduces your confidence. For example, if you are constantly telling yourself that you are unable to speak in front of people, then that is exactly how you will feel. This creates a loop of negativity that will drag all the stressful times from your past right into the present moment. Having a negative inner dialogue will always sow seeds of doubt and knock your confidence down. You will always second guess yourself, which will exacerbate your shyness. Once you realize that you have negative inner dialogue you can turn it around by writing in a journal or mentally stopping your negative thoughts as they occur. Learning how to have a positive inner dialogue will lead to less stressful feelings, such as anxiety, and more confidence in yourself when your shyness is triggered. You will be better equipped to deal with everyday life and overcome your shyness.

Creating Personalized Affirmations to Boost Confidence

The confidence you need to overcome your shyness is not something that you can develop overnight. What is reassuring to know is that even if you don't have that much confidence in yourself it doesn't mean that it will always be this way. You can slowly build up the confidence you need in order to face your shyness head on. Positive affirmations can be used in order to improve areas of self-doubt. They are statements that boost your confidence by reinforcing a positive feature or goal that you would like to achieve for yourself. It doesn't make sense to make bold statements that are far from your reality as your mind may resist something that seems unrealistic; rather it can be helpful to make positive affirmations that build a bridge taking you closer to the goals you would like to achieve. For example, if you are too shy to go on dates to find a suitable partner, a good affirmation would be to say to yourself that "I am working on learning how to connect with others and will soon find a partner who will appreciate me for who I am". Your affirmation should make you feel like you are making small and steady improvements from where you are to where you would like to be. Take the time to analyze the areas where you feel you could use some improvement and tailor some affirmations around them so that you can begin each day by repeating them and reciting them when you feel yourself becoming shy.

In order to create positive affirmations that are effective in helping you overcome your shyness, you need to introspect and discover what your values are. Having affirmations that reinforce your values will create a reward system in your brain that can overcome the shyness that comes when your mind is stressed. According to Mikhail, "The more routinely you affirm a value, the more you exercise the part of your brain that establishes that connection so you can believe it about yourself when you have a challenge" (2022, para 12). Everyday look for at least five things that you are grateful for and reflect upon them; write down your values and goals daily as this firmly imprints them in your mind. Use some of the following statements when crafting your affirmations:

- I am trying to

- I am starting to

- I have learned that

- I am now capable of

- I am working toward

Make sure any statement that you use as an affirmation is something that you truly believe and can see happening for yourself. The more realistic and specific they are, the more your affirmations will help you to overcome your shyness. When you craft your affirmations make sure you get into as much detail as you can. It is not enough to say, "I want to be successful." What would you like to be successful at? Why would you like to be successful? Examples of unrealistic affirmations include saying: "I never feel shy"; "I will make a lot of social connections instantly; I am outspoken." When your positive affirmations are crafted the right way, they will provide a detailed road map of the journey that you are embarking on. They will serve as a constant and steady reminder that though there will be hardships and doubt along the way, if you remain true to your course you will arrive at your desired destination.

Incorporating Daily Affirmations in Your Self-Care Routine

The saying *practice makes perfect* holds water in terms of having a self-care routine. Taking the time each day to assess your mental health and how you feel emotionally is important as it can serve as a vital indicator of areas that you need to focus on. Positive affirmations can be used in your self-care routine to improve your confidence, give your life direction and be a reminder of the person you want to become. In order to imbed your positive affirmations into your mind, you need to incorporate them into your daily routine. Creating a positive habit is doing that habit in the same place at the same time every single day. To use positive affirmations as a part of your self-care routine will reinforce your values and goals and help to ease the emotional difficulties you experience when you are triggered. Commit to the practice of affirmations at least once a day so that they are constantly at the forefront of your mind.

The best time to recite your affirmations is in the morning. If you already have a routine that includes exercise, breakfast and a shower you could insert your daily affirmations right after your exercise session, when your body is chock-full of endorphins. If you don't necessarily have a routine and tend to have rushed mornings, then you could squeeze in your positive affirmations as you brush your hair or teeth in front of the mirror. Where there is a will, there is a way, so I trust that if you truly want to overcome your shyness you will make the necessary time to recite your positive affirmations. It will feel clumsy at first especially if you are saying them out aloud to yourself. There are times where you might feel ridiculous but that is normal. When you truly believe in what you are saying it will start to feel natural and you will begin to look forward to your affirmation time every morning. You can also use your positive affirmations as a sword and shield for the times that you are triggered and feel yourself withdrawing and succumbing to your shyness. Use them in the moment to realign your mind to your values and goals instead of the intimidating situation you find yourself in. Saying your positive affirmations before a challenging situation can help you to overcome shyness and face your fears.

Some people prefer reciting their affirmations out aloud in front of the mirror while others prefer to write them out in their journal. You have to be adventurous enough to explore what will work for you. Do you prefer to recite your affirmations and use verbal repetition? Or perhaps written affirmations are a better fit for you. Some people even prefer to make a recording of their affirmations and listen to it every morning and when they are feeling stressed. You can even mix it up using written or verbal repetition. The choice is really up to you. What I should stress is that the constant and daily repetition of your affirmations is what will reinforce your confidence and create a habit of empowering self-talk. The more you believe what your affirmations are stating, the easier it will be to overcome shyness. Remember to trust the process and put all your faith in what you are saying, and the results will speak for themselves.

Using Visualization Techniques to Reinforce Positive Self-Beliefs

Visualization is a powerful technique when it comes to reshaping how one views themselves. By visualizing certain images, you can actually rewire your mind and how it views specific situations. Numerous coaches actually require their athletes to visualize themselves winning a match or a race as it is known to improve the athlete's performance (Sutton, 2022b). These athletes are coached not only to visualize crossing the finish line, but they are also encouraged to visualize the hard parts of their performance and see themselves overcoming it through mind power and endurance. This can prepare the mind for those difficult parts of their physical performance so that they are not intimidated when those moments arrive. Certain psychological treatments include mental visualization during counseling sessions as a way to treat certain cognitive dysfunctions. Visualizing yourself speaking in front of a room full of people, or whichever situation makes you feel shy, and exhibiting confidence can prepare you for when that moment comes and help you to overcome your shyness. With the aid of visualizations, your brain will not always associate those shy moments with your triggers and will begin to have associations that include you being confident and well-spoken. Visualizations can be a fundamental tool in rewiring your mind to build up your confidence and suppress your shyness.

Get your mind used to visualizations by performing exercises that boost your confidence. You have to create an image of a positive scenario that depicts you being happy and exhibiting outgoing behavior. This is the imagery that will boost your mood and keep stressful feelings at bay. Immersing yourself in this positive scene will also ensure you remain at peace even when you are facing challenging scenarios. In order to practice visualizations, you may follow these steps:

1. Sit or lay in a comfortable position. Close your eyes and take a few deep breaths to calm your body.

2. Visualize all awkwardness and shyness leaving you as you imagine yourself smiling, squaring your shoulder and having good posture.

3. What can you see? What can you hear? How do people in your imagery respond to this new confidence?

4. Relax your entire body as you go deeper in your visualization. Imagine yourself freed from your shyness and all the things that will flow from your new confidence.

5. Let your senses get excited with this new scene as you align yourself to it as your new reality.

6. Continue to breathe deeply and as you inhale, take in more confidence and peace. As you exhale, imagine all negative feelings leaving your mind and body.

7. When you are feeling relaxed and positive, you can open your eyes and return to your life.

You are free to use this visualization technique not only when you start or end the day but also when you are faced with challenging situations. Adding details to the imagery means incorporating sensory details such as smells, sounds, and touch. Furthermore, the more emotion you put into your visualizations, the more effective they will be.

Your inner dialogue dictates how you see the world and your position in it. Taking intentional steps to improve your self-talk while simultaneously harnessing the power of affirmations will improve your levels of self-assurance. By envisioning yourself as a confident, assertive person, you can retreat to this imagery when reminding yourself of what you want to achieve. This imagery will also serve as your refuge when you are in stressful situations that make you want to succumb to shyness. I didn't know how I would ever overcome my shyness; it seemed like a far-fetched dream. My visualizations made my affirmations seem that much more real and I became less afraid until I eventually managed to build up my confidence. I had to stop running from my destiny and embrace new challenges. In the following chapter, I will show just how you can break down the walls of your comfort zone and be the go-getter you have always dreamed of being.

Chapter 3:

Expanding Comfort Zones

The comfort zone is probably a term you have heard of before, but even if you are unfamiliar with it, it is a place you might spend a lot of your time in. Unfortunately, being shy means, you are probably not pushing your boundaries very often. Living your life to the fullest requires you to consistently pursue your dreams and desires. A lot of the time you will have to be in new, and sometimes uncomfortable, positions. This is one of the things I struggled with when I was trying to overcome my shyness. I felt as if being uncomfortable or doing anything outside my comfort zone was detrimental to growth when the opposite was true. I would run from any situation that challenged me; in effect I stayed shy, and my life didn't improve in any way. In this chapter, I will demonstrate why stepping out of your comfort zone can break the inhibiting chains that are created by your timidness. What you will learn is that it is okay to slowly expand the boundaries of your comfort zone so that you can allow yourself to grow and become a better version of yourself so that eventually, you can stop being shy.

Understanding the Concept of Comfort Zones and Their Impact on Shyness

To understand how to step out of your comfort zone, you need to first understand what it is. According to Page, "The comfort zone is a behavioral state within which a person operates in an anxiety-neutral condition, using a limited set of behaviors to deliver a steady level of performance, usually without a sense of risk" (2020, para 8). Since shyness occurs due to feelings of anxiety, self-consciousness, and fear of rejection, the comfort zone becomes a safe haven for those who are shy as they can predict what will happen thus minimizing levels of stress and anxiety. There is nothing wrong with staying in your comfort zone, but it has a limiting effect on your life. By remaining there, you will never transcend your fears and move into the learning and growth zone where you acquire new skills or find your purpose. If you seek the safety of your comfort zone at every turn you will never know what it is like to live to your fullest potential. A growth mindset develops once you bring down your walls and challenge yourself which will boost your personal growth. Forcing yourself to expand the borders of your comfort zone will build your resilience, especially during stressful times. You have more to gain by stepping out of your comfort zone than you have by staying in it.

Strategies for Gradually Expanding Comfort Zones

There is no instant solution for stepping out of your comfort zone. Different methods work for different people. It's important not to rush anything because you don't want to traumatize yourself in the name of growth. It can easily feel suffocating or overwhelming if you do too much too soon. You have to gently coax yourself out of your comfort zone, one task at a time. The first step to take is to set small achievable goals that are designed to have you do things that your shyness usually would stop you from doing. For instance, if you are afraid of making friends or interacting with new people, you could decide to talk to one new person on the bus or at the coffee shop during your commute from home to your job every week. This could be anything from a simple greeting to making a comment about the weather or the service you are receiving. This seemingly small step will rewire your brain to show it that talking to new people is a normal part of everyday life. It will also build your resilience in showing you that sometimes you will spark a vibrant conversation and other times you will be ignored. Both responses are normal.

Take the time to identify the specific areas that your shyness is affecting; this could be your professional career or your love life. You probably have an idea of the things you wish you were doing but are afraid to do because you are scared. Now you have action items under the different areas in your life that your comfort zone is holding you back from. Order your list from the least intimidating action to the one that terrifies you the most. Every week you could choose one area of your life and plan around one action that you want to do within that week. For example, if you are trying to date more, you could identify someone who you're romantically interested in and ask them out for a drink. It helps to have two or three large goals that you break down into smaller manageable goals that you work on on a weekly basis. Overcoming your shyness is like building a muscle; if you don't push it past its limits, it will not grow. Stepping out of your comfort zone requires consistency so breaking your larger objectives to smaller tasks will force you to make an active effort every single day.

Stepping Out of the Comfort Zone and Embracing New Challenges

The most likely reason you will remain in your comfort zone is that you are scared of the unpredictable emotions and experiences you'll experience once you get out of it. Fear is a natural response to situations where you're not able to predict the outcome. Due to this factor of the unknown, you may also tend to doubt if you're making the right decision. Instead of letting your fear and self-doubt overcome you and stop you in your tracks, use it as an indicator that you are pushing your boundaries and getting into the growth zone. Try to calculate the risks and unknowns so that you can try to prevent what may occur; be prepared to also face unpredictable results as that is the nature of life. When you feel scared, adrenaline starts to pump through your blood as this is your body's physical response to fear. Use this adrenaline to face your fears and push yourself beyond what you are comfortable with.

Another way you can overcome your fears is to challenge what you believe. Your uneasiness might be based on something that is not true. Challenge the veracity of the source of your distress. Are you truly bad at public speaking or is this assertion based on the one bad experience you had in middle school? But even if you're not good at speaking in front of people, it is a skill that can be learned. Instead of describing yourself using definitive statements ("I am bad at…", "I suck at…"), change the way you describe yourself by stating that you are getting better every day. Use the following statements to challenge your beliefs:

- "I struggle with making friends but I am improving my social skills."

- "I get anxious when I have to address a crowd of people but I am getting better at controlling my nerves."

- "I feel some self-doubt when I am in social situations but I am building up my confidence and will get better at making connections with others."

When you get your mind in this growth mindset it makes it easier to overcome your self-doubt when you start to feel shy.

The reason your comfort zone even exists is to protect you by creating boundaries when you feel fearful, anxious, and unsure. Unfortunately, when the walls of your comfort zone go up your opportunities dwindle so that what lies beyond it becomes out of reach. Understanding what lies beyond your comfort zone might give you the motivation to step outside of it when the opportunity arises. Along with increased confidence and higher self-esteem, you may also become more creative and develop better problem-solving skills because you encounter different things than you are used to. You may even meet various people with different opinions and backgrounds which will increase your tolerance and strengthen your social skills. In general, when you step out of your comfort zone you will experience more life satisfaction as you take every opportunity to grow. If you don't take the opportunity to push your boundaries your comfort zone can actually stagnate your life. Challenging yourself is uncomfortable but that is the catalyst for growth and self-discovery. It is necessary and quite important to use this discomfort to propel you into a new life.

Celebrating Personal Growth and Accomplishments Outside the Comfort Zone

As I stated previously, it is quite important to be patient with yourself and your progress. You might have been shy for the majority of your life and unlearning that behavior is challenging. Stepping out of your comfort zone is counter-intuitive therefore once you have mapped a way forward, taking that first step is daunting. Once you have taken a small step toward pushing your boundaries you need to acknowledge your progress no matter how small. Perhaps you had told yourself that you would strike up an engaging conversation with your colleague as a small step toward stepping out of your comfort zone and overcoming your shyness. If you only managed to greet your colleague and comment on the weather, it still counts as an achievement because you did something outside your comfort zone. A factor that can often increase self-doubt and reduce confidence is minimizing achievements. Give yourself credit where credit is due. Your brain is more likely to want to do things that provide it with a dopamine (a feel-good chemical) rush. Celebrating and rewarding yourself after taking a step outside your comfort zone can release dopamine in the brain and create feelings of pleasure. In time, your mind will see stepping out of your comfort zone as a good thing.

Having a journal during this journey will make it much easier to track your process. As you make your journal entries on a daily basis, you will explore the different tasks you have done, how they made you feel, and what you plan to do next. If ever you feel like you are stuck and not making any progress, you can page back and reflect on the way you started. It's easy to overlook the progress you made when you are faced with failure but when you look at where you started you will quickly see that you have come a long way. Try and draw lessons from each task that you complete that has pushed you beyond your boundaries. Celebrating each accomplishment allows you to empower yourself with confidence. It is a powerful act to recognize yourself and how competent you are. Even if things didn't go to plan, you realize that whatever you did is worth celebrating and that you will do better next time. Through all your celebration you will gain a new sense of resilience and learn that failure is nothing to be afraid of because it is a steppingstone to growth.

Always remember that all those things can seem challenging or difficult, but it doesn't mean that you will not be able to accomplish them. Expanding your boundaries and pushing yourself beyond what you are comfortable with is one of the most crucial steps to overcoming your shyness. This chapter has given you a few pointers on how to get your journey started and break free of the shackles that are created by your comfort zone. If ever you feel scared or filled with that doubt, it means that you are probably headed in the right direction. You now know practical strategies to slowly expand your comfort zone, how to step outside of your boundaries, and embrace new challenges.

This chapter has also taught you the importance of celebrating personal growth and accomplishments. The fear you once felt may have already started transforming into excitement because you are becoming more resilient as you challenge yourself. Don't forget that the more you expand your comfort zone, the more opportunities you are inviting to enter your life. In the next chapter we will explore what it means to be mindful and more self-aware so you can self-regulate better. When you lead with compassion, you give yourself grace to make mistakes and pick yourself up again. Had I known this before I started my pursuit to overcome my timid nature, I would have saved myself a lot of tears. Being self-aware without placing any judgment on myself moved me so much closer to confidence. I learned that mindfulness allowed me to just be as I was and accept myself. Cultivating that compassion for yourself is the next step on your course to conquer your shyness. Hang in there, we are only just getting started.

Chapter 4:

Mindfulness and Self-

Awareness

Oftentimes when you suffer from shyness, you may also subject yourself to overthinking. I used to pick apart hypothetical situations that had not even occurred yet. My body would break out in sweat and my heart would start to palpitate. I would send myself into an unnecessary frenzy, thinking about things that were beyond my control. Of course, overthinking everything made my shyness a hundred times worse and withdrew even more from social interaction. It wasn't until I learnt the skill of mindfulness that I finally found peace and my mind started to calm down a little bit. I learned different techniques on how to use self-compassion and non-judgmental awareness as essential components in overcoming shyness. This chapter will teach you those different techniques so that you can release yourself from self-judgment and criticism and live a peaceful life.

Practicing Mindfulness to Reduce Overthinking and Self-Doubt

No matter what happens, or what you do, your brain will think. Thoughts are rushing in and out of your mind at lightning speed; it can feel as if you have little control over your mind and what it does. Your mind can sometimes slip into negative patterns of overthinking, and you might find yourself stuck on situations from the past. Rumination occurs when you are obsessing over the future and things that may or may not happen. Overthinking can cause you to doubt yourself especially if you obsess over situations where you failed at certain things. It might cause you to feel as if you are not good enough, especially if you compare yourself to how others handled the same situation. Perhaps your overthinking leads you to shy away from any future contact with other people. When your mind is in this state, the act of overthinking will often fuel your shyness. You should be able to experience a healthy dose of worry without it taking over your life and adding to your stress levels.

According to Frank et al., "Mindfulness has been defined as maintaining a moment-by-moment awareness of our thoughts, emotions, bodily sensations, and surrounding environment with openness and curiosity" (2013, p. 1). When you train your mind to be mindful, you will be less likely to get caught up in overthinking. The present moment awareness that you get from being mindful will allow you to enjoy and be more appreciative of all the things that are happening in the present. There are various mindful techniques that you can use to reduce overthinking such as deep breathing. When you practice breath awareness, you focus on how you are breathing in order to relax your mind and body. Try the following breathing exercise (Lamothe, 2019):

- Find a comfortable seated position and close your eyes.

- Take your right hand and place it on your heart while your left hand is placed on your stomach, just below your ribs.

- Inhale deeply through your nose, pause briefly then allow yourself to exhale through your nose.

- Repeat this for at least five minutes or for as long as you need.

Another technique you can use to stop yourself from overthinking is the body scan. In a quiet relaxed environment, close your eyes and take the time to go over each of your body parts from your head all the way down to your feet. Assess how your body feels and relax where you feel tension. By focusing on relaxation and getting yourself to a more peaceful place you will successfully reduce overthinking.

Cultivating Self-Awareness of Thoughts, Emotions, and Physical Sensations

A large portion of having relationships and interactions with others involves conveying thoughts, feeling emotion and experiencing physical sensations. You do not exist in a vacuum; your social interactions will involve other people. As you speak to one another you will need to form cohesive thoughts that will influence the conversation that you are having. You will have to maintain some level of eye contact and sometimes some physical touch. Throughout these interactions you will be reacting emotionally to what is being said to you and you have to control those emotions in such a way that they are appropriately conveyed through your words. Your thoughts, emotions and sometimes physical sensations are deeply intertwined while you're having any kind of social interaction. They might occur one after the other or simultaneously, but you can almost be sure that you will experience them. If you are not self-aware it can become so difficult to control them or put them into perspective.

Self-awareness is not a skill that comes naturally to some. Sometimes you might be so reactive but not necessarily understand why. In order to understand yourself and the things that trigger you. Introspection requires you to look into yourself to assess how you feel and why. This may not always be a pleasant exercise as you are confronted with feelings you would much rather avoid. One of the most effective ways to introspect is to journal. Writing down events that have happened and how you feel about them will reveal certain patterns and triggers that you may not have been previously aware of. Keeping a journal can also provide you with a track record of your self-awareness journey. Once you have been doing it for some time you can page back and read some of your earlier entries; it may not feel like you have made any progress, but you will notice that you started at a different place and have made progress, no matter how small. Writing in a journal can also be part revealing to you and expose you to emotions you were not even aware of you were feeling.

Another way that you can enhance your self-awareness is to practice mindful exercises often. Due to the fact that being mindful forces you to route yourself in the present moment, you are confronted with your emotions as they unfold. You then have a better idea of how you react in certain situations. This then also gives you information on how to self-regulate when you are faced with triggering situations. When you can anticipate how you will react in certain situations, you can mitigate your emotions and learn how to deal with them before they become overwhelming. It is easier to develop coping mechanisms before the triggering moments occur rather than dealing with heightened emotions that increase your shyness. When you are self-aware you are less likely to feel stressed; self-awareness grants you peace and the ability to enjoy your life as well as making connections with others. Being self-aware plays a critical role in overcoming shyness as you can anticipate the situation that causes you to withdraw into yourself to avoid interacting with others. In your journey to become more confident, I encourage you to develop a better sense of self-awareness so that you can enjoy improved control over your triggers, emotions, thoughts and reactions.

Utilizing Mindfulness Techniques in Social Interactions

Being shy makes having engaging conversations difficult. You might be struggling with your own internal issues so much that you are unable to make the other person you are speaking with feel as if they are important and interesting. Certain mindful techniques can improve your presence in conversations so that you can develop better social skills. Firstly, if you feel your mind wandering during the conversation, do your best to bring it back by focusing on what the person is saying. Take in what they are saying and focus on the details. Secondly, give your full attention to them and stop what you are doing. Do not engage in multitasking during conversations with others; switch off your computer screen or put down your phone so that you can focus solely on what is being said. Thirdly, to show that you are invested in the conversation, ask questions that allow the person you're speaking with to give you more details about what is being said. Avoid asking questions for the sake of it as this may make you seem uninterested. Lastly, take note of the person's body language as it can reveal to you how they feel about the topic at hand. For example, if you are maintaining eye contact and the other person is unable to, it might signify that they are uncomfortable with conversation. Never make assumptions and pause before you speak so that you can think about your response and if it is appropriate. Maintain a non-judgmental approach when you are speaking to others and let their words speak for themselves (Morin & Watkins, 2022).

A technique developed by psychologist Tara Brach is the RAIN acronym which stands for Recognize, Allow, Investigate and Nurture. It is developed in such a way that it will help you to stay in the present moment and have the ability to cope with uncomfortable feelings. RAIN might come in handy for you when you are having conversations with others and start to feel shy. Utilizing the RAIN method means (RAIN: Mindfulness Technique [Worksheet], n.d.):

- R- recognizing where you are, how you feel and the various physical sensations you may be experiencing.

- allow yourself to observe what is happening as an objective party; release any judgment and observe as if you were watching a movie.

- investigate the various thoughts and emotions that you are experiencing; why do you feel that way? What do you need to address your needs?

- N- nurture yourself by providing reassurance and comforting words such as "you are okay," "you are doing well," "I love you." Pretend as if you are giving advice to a loved one. Show yourself kindness and love.

This technique could come in handy when practicing nonjudgmental awareness during conversation. Actively listening to what is being said, absorbing it and giving the appropriate feedback will also improve your social interactions. Shyness might be accompanied by social anxiety therefore staying mindful can help you to face those uncomfortable feelings and navigate social situations better.

Applying Self-Compassion and Non-Judgmental Awareness to Overcome Shyness

Your shyness might be a result of self-doubt which means it is also accompanied by self-judgment and criticism. Your self-criticism and judgment might have a variety of origins such as the messages you receive from society and social media that perpetuate comparisons. This might make you place your value in terms of what you have achieved as compared to your peers. Your self-criticism may also stem from the relationship you have with your family, parents, siblings or caregivers. Unresolved trauma can also influence how critical you are of yourself. According to Foynes, self-compassion can be seen as a "caring response to our own suffering that includes the desire to help ourselves and recognizes that suffering is part of the human condition" (2021, para 54). You deserve self-compassion in order to reduce self-judgment and self-criticism. Because you are a human you will never be perfect; you should always treat yourself with kindness and understanding as your imperfections make you uniquely you. Your shyness is not a weakness. Be objective about this quality that you are trying to improve. You do not need to use self-deprecating or negative labels when referring to your shyness. Self-acceptance and self-compassion go hand in hand when it comes to being kind to yourself. Develop and cultivate those qualities in order to achieve confidence and peace in your life so that you can cope with and manage your shyness. Showing yourself compassion is not a favor you are granting yourself but rather a quality you deserve to experience on a daily basis. Every day on this earth should be one where you are focused on showing yourself kindness, compassion and speaking to yourself with love.

If you have been ashamed in your past due to your shyness, try to work through those emotions and detach your self-worth from that trauma. You have nothing to feel guilty about. There is absolutely nothing wrong with you. In fact, you are probably doing the best you can with the coping skills you have. In reading this book, you are making an attempt to improve your life and that is the best kind of self-love. When I was still grappling with overcoming my shyness, I used to feel ashamed of myself that I couldn't face social situations the same way other people did. I used to feel so much guilt and shame, which made me feel even worse. I called myself all kinds of unpleasant names, such as coward and weak, which further deteriorated my mental wellness. Once I understood that I could overcome my shyness much easier by being kind and not judging myself, I started to vigorously practice self-compassion. I hope the techniques that I have given you in this chapter lead you to a path of self-acceptance and self-compassion. Take your time with it as it took me some time to unlearn how to be harsh with myself. In Chapter 5, you will learn how to be an active listener who is able to engage in active dialogue in an empathetic and supportive way. So, perk up those ears and let's get listening!

Chapter 5:

Active Listening and

Building Connections

When overcoming shyness, you might assume the greatest emphasis should be on how to talk to others when you're feeling shy. This assumption is not necessarily wrong, but it leaves out the importance of listening as well. Good communication encompasses being able to convey ideas and thoughts as well as the ability to listen to what the other party is contributing to the conversation. You should be able to understand the people you are trying to build connections with and a big part of that is active listening so that you can gain better insight into their world. This chapter will give you the tools needed to develop effective listening skills while also being able to engage in active dialogue. Furthermore, I will also discuss what can prevent you from actively listening and provide you with strategies to overcome these challenges.

The Importance of Active Listening in Effective Communication

Active listening is very important for communication as it allows you to show your interest and understanding while you converse with others. According to Cuncic, "Active listening is a communication skill that involves going beyond simply hearing the words that another person speaks but also seeking to understand the meaning and intent behind them" (2022, para 1). When you are actively listening you are taking the time to what is being said verbally as well as any non-verbal cues and giving appropriate responses to show that you understand what is being said and giving the speaker feedback. Being engaged and actively listening will strengthen social connections and interpersonal relationships. It guarantees that you are on the same page as the person you were speaking with, which will reduce any conflict or misunderstandings that may arise from miscommunication. When both parties understand one another's viewpoint, their connection becomes stronger, and they develop a comfortable relationship. In this way, shyness is reduced.

Listening has a positive impact between two people as it boosts their personal connection. When someone is able to rely on the fact that you are genuinely listening to what they are saying and understanding their opinions, then it builds trust between the two of you. This will ultimately strengthen your relationship and create a strong bond between you. Bonding and building trust is an essential component for relationships to thrive whether it is in your personal life or in a professional setting. Active listening makes people feel included and valued which will spark their creativity and allow them to share and be vulnerable. By displaying this quality, you are empowering people, which will boost their self-confidence and self-esteem. When you hear what is being said, without asking any engaging questions, then what you are doing is passive hearing. Signs of passive hearing include daydreaming while someone is speaking, pretending to listen while fiddling with your phone, or nodding without really understanding what the message is. Active listening engages you in what is being said so that you can have a deeper understanding and to give the necessary feedback.

Techniques for Attentive Listening and Showing Genuine Interest

There are various active listening techniques one could adopt and try to perfect in order to develop their active listening skills and they include:

- Listening without a judgment and resisting the urge to give advice.

- Maintaining good eye contact in order to show interest in the conversation.

- Listening to what it said so that you can understand instead of listening to respond.

- Being aware of non-verbal body language and using body language to show interest.

- Paraphrasing and repeating what has been said to ensure there is understanding.

- Immersing yourself in the present conversation and being mindful.

Make sure you have put away all distractions including your phone and minimize any inner dialogue. Make the speaker the pinnacle of your attention and let everything else be a non-priority while they speak. Keep your body language open and not threatening, such as nodding when appropriate, resisting the urge to fold your arms, and having the appropriate facial expression in line with the topic of conversation. Eye contact should be held for 50 to 70% of the conversation; hold the other person's gaze for approximately five seconds and then you can briefly look away. Open-ended questions such as "please tell me more about that" or "what can be done to move forward" can be used to gather more information and keep the conversation flowing smoothly.

To make sure you and the other person you're communicating with are on the same page it can be helpful to practice reflective listening. In this case you will repeat what they have said in order to ensure you have adequately understood how they feel their thoughts and ideas. Repeating what you heard can also offer them validation and make them feel better understood. If you have misunderstood a certain portion of their conversation, then this is an opportunity for them to correct you where you are wrong. Reflective listening captures the essence of the bigger picture instead of sweating the insignificant details. Paraphrasing is a key skill of active listening, but it is important because it shows the other person that you have understood the discussion. Phrases like the ones below a perfect segues during discussions when you want to paraphrase:

- What I understand is…

- Are you saying…

- Am I correct in thinking that…

- I gather from what you have said that…

You can then continue to phrase what they have said into your own words using their key pieces of information. When you do it in this way, they can clarify what they need to and confirm the information that you have got correct. It might take some practice to perfect your active listening skills, but you should be patient with yourself until you feel you have gotten a good grasp of these skills. You might notice yourself having more meaningful conversations or being able to gather more information about those around you once you start putting your listening skills into action. You never know you might even make more friends. To put these skills into action I used to choose one for the day and make myself intentionally use it in every conversation I took part in. For example, if I was practicing my eye-contact I would ensure that I am holding the case of the person I'm speaking with for up to 70% of the time for five seconds at a time. It was intimidating at first but eventually I got it right. You can too if you put enough effort into it.

Building Meaningful Connections Through Active Engagement

Open communication can only take place in a space where both parties are comfortable, neutral, and non-judgmental. Sometimes we don't realize that the environment we have created is not conducive for open communication. For example, because you are struggling with overcoming your shyness you might have given people the impression that you don't want to talk or that you are uninterested in what they have to say. In order to deepen the bonds, you have with the people in your life, make sure that they understand that you will always put their communication as a priority. Checking in frequently to assess how a person feels about their week or emerging development can also make them feel that you support them. When making a comment or giving feedback it should be done in a way to empower that other person. You also have to learn what the other person responds to more as certain people are more verbal while others prefer visual aids. The key is to allow the person to feel as free and comfortable as they can so that you can create a powerful human bond between the two of you.

Sharing is at the foundation of forming deep connections. When another person is able to share with you freely, they will develop a deeper trust in your relationship. As you actively listen to what the other person is saying it is important to ask the right kinds of questions. Closed-ended questions require a 'yes' or 'no' answer that leaves no room for elaboration. These are the kind of questions that you should avoid asking as they don't keep the conversation flowing. A better kind of question to ask is an open-ended question so that the other party can elaborate fully on what they are talking about and offer additional information. For example, if you are having a discussion about their career, you could ask the other person how long they have been in the specific field or why they are so passionate about it. When you ask open-ended questions and probe deeper into what is being said, the other party can see that you are actively listening and taking part in active dialogue which will make the conversation a lot more engaging for them. When you prompt them to share more, they will be encouraged to let down their walls, which will be necessary to foster meaningful connections.

When you converse and actively listen to others you show interest in what they are saying, what is happening in their lives, and how they feel about it. To coax you further out of your shell and to allow you to have meaningful relationships with people around you, you have to show a certain level of curiosity and interest in the lives of other people. Actively listening will create that interest as you explore what makes the other person tick and why they feel the way they do about certain issues. As you learn more about others, you may even realize that your empathy for their situations begins to grow.

Nurturing Relationships Through Empathy, Understanding, and Support

Empathy is described as having the ability to view things from another person's perspective. When you're empathetic you are able to put yourself in that other person's shoes and feel the emotions that they may be experiencing. Empathy is crucial in order to stimulate compassion for others. This skill comes in handy in all situations, both good and bad. For example, if your partner is sick, you might feel uneasy knowing that they don't feel well, and you can try to alleviate their discomfort. Similarly, you may feel bad when your boss has mistreated your colleague and they come to you to share their frustration. When it comes to good news you will have to be just as excited as your friend is when they share that they have gotten a promotion at work or that they are getting married next summer. Some people may use sympathy and empathy interchangeably, but they are not the same thing. Sympathy involves feeling pity for another person whereas empathy allows you to feel the emotions that they are feeling, which evokes compassion instead of pity. Empathy is also a crucial component for forming deeper connections with people around you as it makes them feel valued and understood. When you are empathetic it makes people want to be empathetic towards you, which can also offer you a deeper level of comfort and support.

Developing a strong social network can improve your levels of happiness. Cultivating empathy can serve as the foundation for building this supportive social network that leads to a more satisfying life. Being empathetic can make you want to help others and improve their lives while also reducing conflict. To have an open mind and gain more empathy, you need to understand situations from all sides, not only from your perspectives. Even if someone else's perspective is very different or you don't agree with it, it doesn't make it wrong. People can have experiences and feelings without you passing judgment on them. When your support is non-judgmental, you are in a better place to provide more emotional support to the person you are speaking with. Validating the person, you are speaking with will create a closeness built on trust. The trusting space will also create comfort for you to express yourself and get through your timid nature.

Most people think they are active listeners when there is always room for improvement in the way we interact with one another. You can improve your relationships and how you interact with others by learning various active listening techniques. I realized after learning how to actively listen how much detail I had been overlooking when speaking to my friends and family. My empathy for them grew manifold because I began to notice things I had never picked up on like non-verbal cues and underlying emotions. Active listening allowed me the room to build better relationships with people I already had in my life and a blueprint for those I needed to form connections with. This greatly improved my shyness because I knew what to do in order to be a good listener. By aligning yourself with the techniques in this chapter, you too can forge better connections with those around you.

In the next chapter, I will discuss social anxiety and how to approach certain situations. Of course, if your social anxiety requires you to seek professional help, it is important that you do so. What the following chapter can do for you is to provide you with exposure techniques so that you can cope better in situations that trigger your anxiety. Being able to remain calm when you are in a situation that provokes anxiety is a necessary skill in being able to overcome shyness. Your self-confidence will be less shaky when you are armed with these soothing techniques. So, turn the page and explore how you can be less anxious in social situations.

Chapter 6:

Overcoming Social Anxiety

Your shyness could be just a characteristic you developed as a child due to something that occurred in your past or it could be something deeper such as social anxiety. Social anxiety is a type of anxiety disorder, and it can cripple you when you have to face social situations. If you find yourself avoiding things you have to do at work or at school due to a fear that is sparked by social interactions, you might be suffering from social anxiety. Having this kind of anxiety disorder makes your shyness worse. Your fear of rejection or judgment is amplified, and you might withdraw further into yourself or avoid any kind of social interaction. This chapter will give you some coping strategies when you feel overwhelmed and social situations. Although you may need professional help to overcome your social anxiety if it is severe, this chapter will give you some exposure techniques that will desensitize you to situations that would otherwise make you feel anxious.

Understanding Social Anxiety and its Relation to Shyness

It is quite important to understand what social anxiety is and how it differs from regular shyness. According to National Institute of Mental Health:

> A person with social anxiety disorder feels symptoms of anxiety or fear in situations where they may be scrutinized, evaluated, or judged by others, such as speaking in public, meeting new people, dating, being on a job interview, answering a question in class, or having to talk to a cashier in a store (2022, para 3).

When you suffer from social anxiety, you might experience intense feelings of self-consciousness that alter the way that you live your life. The worry about what people might think about you is intense and it can even consume you. Being shy might just be that hesitant feeling that you get when you are put in a social situation. Shyness is not seen in the serious light as social anxiety, as shyness is simply a minor case of social discomfort. Basically, shyness is not as consistent and intense as social anxiety. When you are shy you might still be able to overcome your distress and carry on with your life. Social anxiety puts you in a constant state of suffering that is not easy to overcome and might even manifest in physical symptoms such as panic attacks, nausea, or profuse sweating.

The exact causes for social anxiety disorder are not known but there are various factors that have been identified that can contribute to a person developing social anxiety. A big risk factor is that it may be hereditary. There is no conclusive proof as to why certain family members develop social anxiety while others enjoy a normal social life. More research needs to go into how the brain and body work when people with social anxiety disorder are interacting with other people. In order to provide support for yourself or to another person who may be suffering from social anxiety disorder you need to first educate yourself on what the disorder entails as well as what treatment options are available. You should be able to adequately communicate your symptoms to a loved one and what you are struggling with. If you are feeling overwhelmed by your symptoms, then it is best to seek help and speak to a professional.

Coping Strategies for Managing Social Anxiety in Various Situations

Sometimes the cause of social anxiety stems from negative inner dialogue and thoughts. In order to identify and challenge these negative thoughts and beliefs you might have to partake in certain activities that will reveal them to you. Firstly, you might try being mindful so that you are alert and can catch it when this negativity arises in real time. Pay attention to your thoughts and when self-critical statements arise challenge them with a positive fact about yourself. Secondly, you could keep a record of your thoughts, how they made you feel as well as what triggered them. Thirdly, be wary of cognitive distortions; these are biased thoughts that create negative thought loops. Taking things personally all the time, mind reading and making assumptions, all-or-nothing thinking, and catastrophizing are some examples of cognitive distortions. Identifying the ones that apply to your life could help you to challenge the root of your negative thoughts. In order to cope with social anxiety, you have to implement certain relaxation techniques so that you are not consumed by your negative emotions.

With certain relaxation techniques, you can get your mind to a neutral state where it can discern which fears are real and which are manufactured to torment your mind. Try the following breathing exercise:

1. Find a quiet and comfortable place to either sit or lay down where you will not be disturbed.

2. Close your eyes and take in a deep slow breath with your nose, making sure to engage your diaphragm.

3. When your lungs are full and you can no longer take him any more air, hold your breath for a few seconds.

4. Proceed to exhale slowly using your mouth as the air is forced through pursed lips. Imagine anxiety and stress leaving your body.

5. Repeat as many times as is needed as you force your body to relax where it is holding tension.

Another exercise that could help relieve anxiety is progressive muscle relaxation. It can be practiced in the following manner:

1. Find a comfortable room that is quiet and spacious where you can sit or lay down.

2. Choose a specific body part or muscle group such as your shoulders or hands and tense them for a few seconds.

3. Release the tension completely and allow that body part to completely relax and to become loose.

4. Repeat a few times and notice how your muscles feel once the tension is relaxed.

5. Try to work your way through each muscle group from the top of your head to the tips of your toes.

These exercises could be performed at the beginning and end of each day, and also during moments of stress when you feel overwhelmed.

Developing coping mechanisms to alleviate the symptoms of social anxiety is crucial in your journey to overcome shyness. Simple activities like positive self-talk or visualization can help to calm you down and challenge your negative patterns. Instead of thinking that everybody will laugh at you when you deliver your speech you could try to change the narrative and say "I am capable and competent, what I have to say is important. I add value to my society." To reinforce productive imagery, you could visualize yourself making the speech successfully and the crowd erupting in applause because they are so impressed with what you said.

Seeking Professional Help for Severe Social Anxiety

Sometimes your social anxiety is beyond any self-help methods. You should be able to recognize the signs when your social anxiety becomes severe and requires professional intervention. When your social anxiety starts to interfere with the daily running of your life such as you going to work or school or attending social events, then it may need some professional attention. If you go out of your way to avoid any social interactions, then that is a warning sign as well. When you experience physical symptoms, like sweating, heart palpitations, trembling, shortness of breath, nausea and vomiting, as well as experiencing severe emotional distress then it is likely that your social anxiety is out of control. When your self-confidence and self-esteem have taken a dive and you cannot seem to shake your negative self-perception, you may have to consult a mental health professional to help you turn things around.

When you turn to professionals for help, they may use a variety of methods to help you cope with your social anxiety. A common method used to overcome social anxiety is therapy and counseling. Cognitive behavioral therapy allows an individual to introspect and reveal negative thoughts as well as develop healthy coping strategies through exposure therapy. In essence, you will be reshaping your thoughts and building your confidence at the same time. When you go for therapy, the therapist might help you to learn certain social skills and effective communication practices that can help you thrive in social interactions. On top of that they will give you the emotional support that you need in order to comfortably express how you feel your fears and concerns when it comes to your social anxiety. The majority of the time therapists time travel all the way back to your childhood and unpack the issues and underlying causes. If the therapist sees fit, they may prescribe medication to help ease the symptoms of your social anxiety. Anti-Anxiety medications like benzodiazepines and serotonin reuptake inhibitors are usually prescribed by psychiatrists if they feel it may help to alleviate your social anxiety symptoms. Complementary medicine can also be prescribed if it can provide additional support in your healing.

Gradual Exposure Techniques to Desensitize Yourself to Anxiety-Provoking Social Situations

When dealing with social anxiety gradual exposure is a common therapeutic technique that is utilized in order to alleviate symptoms. What it involves is to slowly and gradually expose the person with social anxiety to the feared situation in a controlled environment. The goal of this is to desensitize the person and help them to develop resilience and a new response to their fears. According to the American Psychological Association, "When people are fearful of something, they tend to avoid the feared…situations. Although this avoidance might help reduce feelings of fear in the short term, over the long term it can make the fear become even worse" (2017, para 1). When dealing with social anxiety, gradual exposure can be helpful because the fear that the sufferer imagines in their mind is never as bad as it is in reality. Exposing them to their fears will help them to realize that things are really not as bad as they think. There are various ways that you could enact gradual exposure such as the in vivo approach where you face your fears directly. Another approach is the imaginal exposure where you use visualizations to face your social anxiety. Virtual reality exposure can come in handy if the person is not able to carry out in vivo exposure. Interoceptive exposure may be brought on by using physical sensations that are feared to demonstrate that there is no harm in them.

Perhaps another helpful activity is creating a hierarchy of anxiety-provoking situations to guide exposure therapy. You can order these situations from the least anxiety-provoking to the most anxiety-provoking. You would begin by starting with the less intense situation and seeing how you would fare in that scenario. Gradually you would face more challenging situations as a way to face your fears and overcome your social anxiety. The secret is in continually exposing yourself to triggering situations and finding ways to cope with them. In that way you will build resilience against the things that you had thought you could never face.

Social anxiety can be a crippling disorder that dampens your quality of life. Due to the shyness that I experienced in my life, I used to think that I had social anxiety. Fortunately, my shyness wasn't as extreme as this anxiety disorder. You might be the same as me or you may actually be struggling with social anxiety. I am not a doctor, and I am not able to diagnose you. What you need to do is speak to a medical professional and explain to them what you experience when you are faced with social interactions. They have the expertise to make an assessment and a referral if necessary. Being diagnosed with social anxiety doesn't mean you can't live a satisfying and meaningful life. You can learn to cope with your mental disorder and still overcome the shyness that comes with it. This chapter has given you the tools to recognize what social anxiety is and what to do when the symptoms start to overwhelm you. Once you understand how social anxiety presents itself and how limiting it is, you can take the steps mentioned in this chapter to desensitize yourself to its effects. At some point you may get it under control enough to start networking. When you reach that point, the next chapter will be your guide on how to build up your professional connections.

Chapter 7:

Networking and Building

Professional Relationships

Being shy by nature can hinder your ability to progress in your professional career. To thrive in a professional setting, there are certain skills you need to have. You will need to be able to connect with other people in order to network and expand your professional skills. You have to be able to clearly articulate yourself not only when you're motivating for improvements in the way things are done but also when you are seeking growth opportunities and promotions within the company. At the very core of professional relationships is a connection between two people based on the exchange of expertise and knowledge. Being shy might prohibit you from fully carrying out these tasks that could propel your career forward in the right direction. This chapter gives you the necessary steps you need to take in order to put your shyness aside and learn how to network and build meaningful professional relationships.

I used to think that my work would speak for itself and that I didn't need to say anything more to get myself ahead. Boy was I wrong! I could've probably gotten ahead in my career without doing anything else but working hard but it was going to take a lot longer. I then discovered that there was a shortcut I could take but it would involve working through my shyness and learning how to network. The talk seemed daunting but to me I knew I had to do it if I was truly going to go far. Slowly, I learned how to self-promote and showcase my skills so that people would notice me and help me if opportunities arise. I had to become visible so that I didn't fade into the background. Although you may be good at what you do you might appear as a part of the furniture because your shyness stops you from standing out. You might even be the right person for a vacant leadership role, but your superiors may mistake your reserved nature for a lack of confidence and assertiveness. If you are tired of being overlooked in the workplace because you are too shy to put yourself at the forefront, this chapter is for you.

Strategies for Networking in Professional Settings

Networking has become a buzzword in the professional world and for good reason. To network is to form beneficial professional relationships with other people in the same industry or line of work. In order to take your career development seriously, you have to put a considerable effort into networking. Once established, your network serves as your support system, guiding and uplifting you during work-related crossroads and dilemmas. In terms of career advancement your network could be essential in revealing new skills you should acquire all positions that open up that you might be interested in. There are many ways to nurture your network from attending conferences and conventions to subscribing to the relevant social media platforms to keep up to date with industry changes and development. What you should remember is that the work you put into it is what you will get out. Networking is an investment. Putting in the right kind of effort can yield results that transform your career for decades to come.

There are different ways that you could take advantage of the networking opportunities that are relevant to you, such as joining a networking group. Within these groups are professionals from different industries that may have a clearer idea on how to establish new relationships with others. Join professional social media platforms that allow you to increase the amount of work-related connections that you have. Due to the fact that other professionals that you have worked for in the past may be on the same kind of platform, you can have a reference history that is easily accessible online. Create and maintain a database of contacts so that you can easily obtain information for specific people who are seeking advice. Frequent conventions and conferences that are relevant to your industry and try to participate as much as you can—attend the talks, sign up for newsletters, and exchange contact information. It is helpful to walk around with a pocket full of business cards to hand out to anyone who is willing to take it. Sending introductory emails provides an opportunity for you to connect with the receivers of the email. You can also outline when they should reach out to you or emphasize that you are always there to help.

Striking up a conversation with someone in the same professional field can be sparked by current professional news and developments. Approach that individual in a relaxed way and make a comment about something that they are engaged in or an interesting development that has recently occurred in your field. Wait for their response and engage in lighthearted banter about the topic. Once they seem comfortable with you, introduce yourself, where you work, and what role you play in that establishment. Ask the person about what they do and where they work. Transition into asking them if they would like to collaborate or work together in the future. Being inquisitive about what they do while also sharing information about your own career can reap results that you didn't expect even at the first meeting. Once the connection has been established make sure that you check on the person often either via email or social media. Invite them to relevant industry events and let them know that you are available to attend any events that they may be attending. It is not enough to simply create connections, you have to nurture them and grow them to be a consistent and stable part of your work life.

Building Rapport and Connections for Career Advancement

When you are in the professional world there is a certain way that you should carry yourself in order to build rapport with others in such a way that they will help you in your career advancement. You have to be present and attentive. Make sure you maintain the right amount of eye-contact while focusing on the person you're speaking with. Do not succumb to any distractions around you such as your phone or computer so that you are able to be fully present in the conversation. Ask the other person open-ended questions to demonstrate your curiosity in their professional experiences. Use of reflective listening skills to paraphrase and summarize what the person has just said in order to show them that you're paying attention and have understood the gist of what they are saying. If there are any misunderstandings, then it gives the person a chance to get them cleared up right away and carry on with the conversation. Before sharing your experiences, make sure the other person has had ample time to fully outline the things that they have gone through. Avoid interrupting them and trying to put the focus on you. Show empathy where relevant and validate their experience by acknowledging any tenacity or courage they showed during their professional career. Try to always remember specific details about each individual that you can bring up in any subsequent conversations; this will make them feel like you listen intently and truly value them.

The kind of relationships you build with other people should be the ones that you genuinely enjoy. According to Martins, "Rapport is an essential soft skill to help you build trust, establish effective communication, and develop great relationships with your team members" (2023, para 1). Having a good rapport with the people you work with simply means that you are able to make the other people feel as if they are valuable while they too make you feel seen and heard. Building rapport with your colleagues is essential to strengthen the bond between team members and boost loyalty. There will be mutual trust between members, and they will feel as if they are bringing unique value to the team. When a team is in sync and has a good group dynamic, they are better able to achieve company goals and targets. Establishing a synergetic rapport ensures that everyone is on the same page and can communicate effectively with one another. It is essential to keep connections alive by consistently checking on the other person and following up on their well-being and career. When you are on the same social media platforms it is easy to see when this individual has been promoted or has started working for a new company. Make comments on these advancements, congratulate them or ask if you can help with anything. As you keep checking in, the other person will feel as if you are genuinely interested in their success. They may also take a genuine interest in your career advancement and help you to achieve certain professional goals.

Overcoming Shyness in Job Interviews and Professional Networking Events

When you start to enjoy the fruits of your networking efforts and get offered a job interview or you are invited to networking events, you have to prepare yourself mentally and physically to succeed. Getting ready to face an interviewer is very important as you need to present yourself confidently in order to make a good impression. You can follow these strategies to come out on top:

- Researching the company and the job role: Familiarize yourself with the company's values and mission statement as well as any recent news. Get yourself up-to-date with current industry trends. Doing this will show them that you are invested in their establishment.

- Prepare a list of common interview questions and practice answering them. Always include a specific example in any of your answers.

- Try to familiarize yourself with the job role and requirements so that you can demonstrate that your skills are in alignment with it.

- Learn how to summarize your experiences and capabilities in a way that exhibits adequate self-assessment skills.

- Create an elevator pitch about who you are in the professional world and what your experience and future entails. Practice this elevator pitch with enthusiasm and confidence.

- Keep your body language open and dress appropriately. When you look good in your professional outfit, it not only boosts your confidence but it also gives the impression that you are a respectful person.

It is important to maintain a good attitude as you walk into the interview room. If your shyness is overwhelming you, try to turn it into excitement or anticipation of what is to come. Visualize yourself doing well during the interview. Utilize positive affirmations such as "I am competent," "I will do well during the interview" to boost your confidence and ease your anxious feelings. Remember to use deep breathing exercises if you need to relax. A positive mindset can do wonders for the success of your job interview.

Leveraging Networking Opportunities for Personal and Professional Growth

Before you start networking, it is important to set some goals for your networking activities. What is it that you would like to achieve? To define clear objectives for your networking activities will give you defined actionable steps that you need to take in order to succeed. Decide what your area of interest is and gather information around it. Check what the history is and where the industry is going. Set some networking goals as per your interests and research. They should fall in line with your long-term career goals. Using the SMART goals technique, make sure your goals are Specific, Measurable, Achievable, Realistic, and Time-Bound. An example of a networking goal is to make three connections with professionals in the same industry and meet with each of them at least twice within the next month to learn about their experience, insights, and skills. Once your goals are defined, the next step is to break your goal up into actionable steps. Based on the above example your next steps could be, seek out professionals in my field, introduce myself and connect and set a follow-up meeting. Be flexible and pivot when plans do not go your way. If someone is not able to meet, reschedule. Do not feel discouraged when someone is busy.

Getting a mentor to guide your career could also allow you to proceed in the right direction even if you struggle with being shy. A mentor is someone in the same field who has achieved the things you dream of achieving. As you admire them in the way they carry themselves, their achievements, and where their career is, it can be inspiring to have them shape your career. Surround yourself with people who have more industry knowledge than you do and you will have so much to learn. You would be surprised how many experts are eager to share their expertise with people in the same field. After doing the appropriate research and identifying the ideal possible mentors, reach out to them to make introductions. Propose a mentoring arrangement where you outline the frequency of meetings and what will be discussed.

After getting a mentor within the organization I worked for, they guided me on how to expand my skill set and climb up the corporate ladder in a way that made me the undeniable choice every time an opportunity arose. I thought I could do it on my own but that was my shy nature taking over my mindset. My mentor forced me out of my comfort zone so I couldn't use my shyness as an excuse. They changed my life for the better and I hope you will get to experience something similar.

Your shyness is likely holding you back and robbing you of emerging possibilities in your life. Use this chapter to improve your networking skills and create a career path that is destined for nothing but greatness. In the next chapter, I will help you to explore connections with other people in this rapidly changing digital era. The world is accelerating toward digitization, and you need to learn how to navigate both the online and offline world without letting your shyness run rampant.

Turn the page on analogue and plug into this new world.

Chapter 8:

Socializing in a Digital Age

It may seem as if the internet is a beneficial tool that can be used to help shy people bloom and connect with others. Although this is somewhat true you have to know how to navigate online communities as a shy person and translate that into offline connections. This is not always simple to do. This chapter will give you some techniques on how to balance your digital connections with those you have in-person. I used to rely on online connections to fill my lack of real life, in-person connections. Somehow no matter how many online connections I made, it still didn't fill the void. I still felt lonely. That is because I have not yet learned how to balance online relationships with those I have with people in my regular life. It's easy to fall into this trap when you are shy because you don't know how to connect with people around you. With some assistance you can now Connect with people on and off the computer.

Navigating Social Interactions in the Digital Age

It is almost impossible to avoid socializing on a digital platform. There are so many different social media platforms that you can choose to use, depending on your preference. Some people prefer TikTok over Facebook or Instagram over Twitter. There are certain dynamics at play when using digital platforms to communicate and form connections. According to OECD:

> Inequalities along age, gender, and socio-economic lines in the use of digital technologies mean that certain groups are better able at using digital technologies for higher well-being outcomes in many dimensions, such as jobs and income, health, work-life balance and social connections (2019, para 1).

Without even realizing it, the glorified digital transformation may not have the same effect on people in developing countries as those who have resources readily available like in developed countries. Although the digital age has a higher chance of giving more people opportunities to improve their quality of life and well-being, it also presents a risk of widening inequalities. When navigating digital platforms, you need to also have social and emotional skills that will allow you to benefit from any interactions online. In this way you are able to avoid situations that may affect your mental health negatively.

There is a social media platform for everybody. You could use Facebook, where you can create communities based on common interests or Instagram that focuses more on using digital images to connect people. Perhaps you fancy the micro-blogging platform that is Twitter or maybe you are a gamer who prefers to connect with the gaming community on Twitch. The social media platform you choose should align to your interests and desires. Digital socialization allows you to connect with a vast number of people, which gives you access to a large support network. You get exposed to different and diverse perspectives as you interact with people from different cultures. You are also able to connect with others at any time regardless of physical location. The downside is that there is limited face-to-face interaction, and this can compromise the quality of the relationship. Another disadvantage is that you are exposed to cyber bullying and harassment that can negatively affect your mental health. It is also quite easy to get addicted to digital socialization and it can consume a lot of your time that could be used for other constructive activities. During digital socializing, your personal information could be shared online, which raises privacy and security concerns.

Overcoming Shyness in Online Communities and Social Media Platforms

Although online interactions have a certain anonymity to them you may find that you still experience shyness. There could be several contributing factors such as:

- previous negative experiences online could serve as a deterrent to connecting with others on a digital platform.

- you being unable to read body language and non-verbal cues that help you to adequately communicate with others.

- you being afraid of what the online community might say or what people might think should they discover your online activity.

Therefore, contrary to popular belief, you may still experience shyness even when communicating on a digital platform. Just because being behind a screen might lower the inhibitions of most people, there is no guarantee that it will lower your inhibitions.

You can practice how to express yourself online by slowly building up your confidence. It may take practice, patience, and self-acceptance but it is a real possibility. You can start by expressing your opinion on non-contentious online platforms such as gardening groups or cooking forums. As time goes on you will start to feel comfortable expressing your opinion no matter the topic of conversation. Try to remind yourself of your strengths and the things that you have achieved when you start to doubt yourself. understand that not everybody will agree with your perspective and that is okay. As you accept yourself, you will also come to embrace your individuality and that your opinions may be rejected or supported. Align yourself with communities that are supportive and that will encourage you to express yourself. If you are still struggling to jump into the conversation you can use the following tips:

- Participate in conversations that genuinely interest you and share your reactions and opinions.

- Point out the things you have in common with the person you are trying to connect with online.

- Remember to use multimedia such as an image, video, or GIF in order to make your content more engaging.

- Keep an open mind and be receptive to feedback.

By using these simple tips, you can learn how to easily strike up a conversation with somebody who seems interesting on a digital platform. You might not expect your shyness to rear its ugly head but if you know how to anticipate it, you can still type away and forge meaningful connections without skipping a beat.

Balancing Digital and In-Person Socialization for a Well-Rounded Social Life

In order to thrive in life, you need to be able to strike a balance between your digital and your face-to-face interactions. While your digital life allows you the benefit of reaching out to niche communities and people who share the same interests as you, real life interactions give you that deeper emotional connection because the person is physically in front of you, and you can reach out and touch them. Both types of socializations have their pros and cons, but you cannot have a fulfilling social life if you neglect one of them. Choosing to live without digital socialization robs you of the opportunity to access certain support networks when you are in crisis. Likewise, if you decide not to have face-to-face interactions with other people you risk not developing adequate social skills that will help you thrive in your community. You can't have one without the other and in order to have a balanced social life you should be able to navigate online platforms while also keeping your real-life connections deep and meaningful.

In order to strike a healthy balance between online and offline interactions you should consider setting clear boundaries that will dictate when you are online and when you are offline. Make in-person interactions a priority in your life and do not use your phone during face-to-face conversations so that you can give the person your undivided attention and adequate eye-contact. Don't forget to take some time away from digital platforms once in a while so that you can detach yourself from your online persona and activities to focus on off-line goals in your day-to-day life. When you are online try to practice mindful online activity; choose only activities that allow you to be productive and achieve your goals. Avoid mindlessly scrolling through social media and comparing your life to others. Balance your passive online activities (reading articles, watching videos) with your active engagement such as commenting on conversations. You should try to create as much content as you consume. Develop new offline hobbies that keep your life interesting and fulfilling.

You should try to take advantage of each type of socialization in order to improve your life. Digital media should be used to expand your network and allow you to engage with like-minded people. You can further push your creativity or professional knowledge by sharing and collaborating with the relevant parties. You can even build your own inclusive spaces that reach a diverse audience, that are governed by shared interests and mutual respect. Digital media can be used to find mentors and expand on your personal growth and development. On the other hand, socializing in person allows you to practice your active listening and empathy in order to build a foundation of trust. There is nothing that beats that face-to-face interaction with another human being or that group dynamic when multiple people are bonding at the same time. When you are meeting with people in person you have the opportunity to create a welcoming and safe environment for them that allows them to express themselves. Being aware of the advantages of each digital media can help you to strike a better balance.

Cultivating Online Relationships and Translating Them into Offline Connections

Sometimes your online activity leads to a connection that you did not expect. If you are able to form a connection on an online platform with another person, then it will probably become important for you to nurture that online relationship and try to transition it to become an offline connection. Things get a little shaky when you move the relationship from the online space to the offline reality. The first important thing to remember is to keep your communication active and give thoughtful responses. Don't reply for the sake of replying. Be thoughtful and empathetic. Secondly, try to switch things up and include video calls or send voice chats when you can. Using different kinds of media can break the monotony of sending text messages. Lastly, try to celebrate important milestones and achievements such as birthdays, anniversaries, promotions, or graduations so that the person can feel like you are invested in their development. When you put the right kind of effort in, the person that you are maintaining a relationship with on the digital platform can feel as fulfilled as they might if it was an offline connection. If an opportunity to meet arises, should you take it or should you leave the relationship on an online platform?

Before meeting somebody that you encountered online, ensure that you have taken necessary safety measures, such as sharing your location with a trusted loved one and meeting in a public place. You can try to meet at a conference or convention that is related to your shared interest. If you are traveling to a location that is near your online connection, you can notify them in advance and meet them at a local tourist attraction. You can invite them to a networking event that is important to you so that they can watch you in your professional element. You don't have to force a moment like this to arrive as it will probably occur naturally. If you sense some apprehension from the other person do not force them to meet with you. It is advisable to highlight the importance of meetings in order to deepen your connection. A simple thing to remember is to stay consistent. Even if you successfully transition to an offline relationship with the person, you met online, you should still do the things that forged your connection in the first place. Try to maintain your texting frequency so that they feel included in your life. Now that the relationship has evolved into an offline one, you should prioritize your face-to-face time and make plans to see each other often.

Online connections can be just as fulfilling as the offline ones, you just have to be discerning as to which ones will benefit you and which ones won't. Learning how to socialize in the digital age is a must and it can help you to overcome your shyness. Regardless of where you are socializing, you will still need to also learn how to maintain your boundaries so that you can feel safe and comfortable in who you are. If that sounds like an uphill battle, please turn the page because I have all the leverage you need in the next chapter.

Chapter 9:

Maintaining Boundaries

and Assertiveness

For some people, setting boundaries and being assertive is something that comes naturally to them. They do not struggle with how to bring up the topic and often flag violations when they occur. This may not be your reality. You may struggle with vocalizing what your boundaries are or addressing individuals who have violated your boundaries. Being shy can cause you to shrink and freeze when someone oversteps your boundaries. Later on, you may feel guilt and shame that you were not able to stand up for yourself in the moment. I used to be in the exact same position. I was not able to speak up when people would cut in front of me in the coffee shop. I could not confront my colleague who always seemed to eat my snacks without asking for permission or apologizing for the inconvenience. Even when someone close to me said something about me that was untrue, I was not able to correct them or challenge their version of events. I was often frustrated not only with the people who violated my boundaries but also with myself. Until I learned how to overcome my shyness and assert my boundaries, people kept walking all over me. In this chapter, you will learn how to be more assertive and communicate your boundaries authoritatively.

Setting Personal Boundaries to Protect Oneself From Being Taken Advantage of

To learn how to set your boundaries, you need to first understand what personal boundaries are. According to Sanok:

> Boundaries are limits we identify for ourselves, and apply through action or communication. When we define what we need to feel secure and healthy, when we need it, and create tools to protect those parts of ourselves, we can do wonders for our well-being at work and at home—which, in turn, allows us to bring our best selves to both places (2022, para 1).

Boundaries are significant in our lives as they allow us to create a space where we can feel secure and at peace. When this sense of peace prevails, we can then let the best parts of ourselves shine. With boundaries you are sending a message to your friends, colleagues, and family about how you wish to be treated.

To identify what your boundaries are specifically you may need to assess what your values are as well as your needs and limits are. Hard boundaries are things that you are not willing to compromise on such as personal space or violence. Soft boundaries are things that you are flexible with and can compromise on that are not tightly tied to your values and needs. Ascertaining what your hard and soft boundaries are gives you a blueprint for establishing clear boundaries. When your boundaries are violated, you will often feel guilt or shame or that you should have said no in that situation. In that instance a person may not react well to you saying no to them but remember that it is not your place to soothe people when they feel uncomfortable with your decision. When you recognize that your boundaries have been violated it is important to be mindful in the moment and take a step back to reassert your limits. When you realize that your boundaries have been crossed, it is helpful to remove yourself from the situation and plot a way forward that reinstates your limits.

Developing Assertiveness Skills to Express Needs and Opinions Confidently

Being assertive allows you to express what you need and how you feel in a confident manner. You are able to express your own feelings while considering those of other people. When you are acting assertively you are able to maintain your position without being swayed by others' emotions and less faced with facts to the contrary. On the other hand, passive behavior is where a person allows another's opinions and ideas to override theirs. When you are being passive you avoid conflict and may phrase your concerns as questions instead of statements. Passive behavior often leads to pent up feelings that are not expressed and can lead to anxiety, depression, or fear. People sometimes confuse assertiveness with aggressiveness. Being assertive is not aggressive at all. When you behave in an aggressive manner you often violate another person's boundaries in order to dominate them and get your way. Aggressive behavior was often abusive, hostile, and confrontational; an aggressive person will put down your feelings and ideas in order to make theirs seem better. They often intimidate or belittle others. When a person behaves in this way it is often misplaced and stems from trauma in their past. This kind of behavior often disrupts the synergy in a team and breeds hostility among colleagues.

Self-confidence and high self-esteem are necessary in order to be assertive. Self-confidence is having a positive view of yourself and what you are capable of in terms of your strengths and weaknesses. On the other hand, self-esteem is the value that we place on ourselves in terms of how we value ourselves and how we feel people value us. Having a strong sense of self and knowing who you are allows you to know what you believe in and what you will and will not tolerate. Knowing how valuable you are and that you do not need to compromise for anybody can help you better assert yourself when you need to stand your ground. When negative thoughts about yourself arise you can challenge the veracity and counter them with positive assertions. This is something that you may have struggled with due to the fact that you are shy by nature. Fortunately, being shy doesn't mean that you can't learn how to improve your self-esteem and self-confidence in order to be able to stand up for yourself.

There are certain things you can practice in order to be more assertive, such as:

- Using *I* statements instead of passing criticism. "I don't agree," or "I feel differently" instead of saying "You don't know what you are talking about."

- Learn how to say no without explaining why you were saying no. The word no is a complete sentence. Say it firmly.

- Keep your body language in sync with what you are saying. Remember to keep a straight back and maintain eye contact; do not cross your arms.

- Don't be afraid to practice what you want to say out loud in front of a mirror as if you are role-playing.

- Regulate your emotions even if conflict occurs. Take deep breaths and remain calm. Try to keep your voice steady.

You can use these techniques to communicate assertively and express how you feel and what you think. The leap from being shy to becoming assertive is quite a big one so remember to start slow and small then build your way up from there.

Balancing Assertiveness With Empathy and Respect for Others

Being assertive does not mean you act on your own feelings without considering those of other people. You do not live in a vacuum nor do your feelings matter more than other people's feelings. No man is an island. You have to live peacefully side-by-side with other people even as you accept your opinions and feelings. Not everybody will think the way that you do because they have had different life experiences than you have. Even a romantic partner may have differing perspectives and feelings. While you are learning how to be assertive you should also consider that people need to also feel validated in opinions and emotions even if you don't necessarily agree with their viewpoints. The basis of strong and fulfilling relationships is the exchange of ideas and opinions; if you don't take the time to hear what other people think then it is not likely that the connection will be forged. How will you know what you have in common with others if you don't recognize how they feel and what their stand is on various issues? Your feelings and values are important in the same way that other people's feelings and values are. You need to strike a balance between asserting how you feel and respecting the feelings of other people.

Actively listening to what people are saying (as I have outlined in Chapter 5) is important in order to identify what other people may need. Understanding their concerns can build empathy for their plight. Having empathy for other people and what they need allows you to know where their limits are and how to respect their boundaries. You cannot expect people to respect your boundaries while you are trampling all over theirs. Maintaining your empathy for others when you interact with them can help you to strike a healthy balance between being assertive with your feelings and understanding their viewpoints. Meaningful relationships are give and take. On some days you will be in the party that shares and needs support while the other party is quiet and understanding. On other days, the roles will be reversed, and you will need to be compassionate and respectful to what the other party is going through. You have to know when it is important to back down and when you have to be assertive with your feelings. Sometimes it is crucial to say something and stand firm and other times it is not that important. So the next time you plan on being assertive, you should add a little empathy and think about the other person in the situation: what are they saying; how do they feel about everything; is there any way you can make it better; are they triggered by something that happened or what you said? step into the shoes and try to understand why they feel the way they do in that moment.

Strategies for Effective Communication and Boundary Maintenance in Different Contexts

The way you communicate is very important as it helps to avoid misunderstandings and conflict. Various settings have different communication styles that differ from one another; the way you communicate at home will be vastly different from the way you communicate in your workplace. Being assertive in a professional setting may require you to say no to certain things that will derail you from your core duties. In that scenario and using a formal tone, you should set some time to meet with your line manager to let them know that although you were excited to be a part of the project, you unfortunately cannot take it on with your existing workload. It would be helpful to explain that the extra load will compromise the quality of your work. In a personal capacity, you may not like the way your partner speaks to other people. You might have to let them know that this makes you feel uncomfortable as it seems that they are comfortable disrespecting other people. Although you don't want to hurt their feelings, you might still have to express to them that their behavior is problematic. You can let them know that it makes you uncomfortable when they speak to other people that way as it reflects badly on them. Explain further that you value respect as a basic human trait and it is important that you're with somebody who respects other people. In a social setting you may have to explain to your friend why they cannot date your brother, for example. Your communication style in this respect will be quite casual but you will still have to explain that your friendship with them may be tarnished if their relationship goes badly. Explain kindly that you would prefer if they didn't date your sibling as that would make you feel uneasy.

Try to recognize your own feelings and where you are having issues with being assertive. Self-introspection can lead you to discovering the things you enjoy, what makes you feel good and the areas that stress you out or things that you are apprehensive about doing. The areas you tend to automatically become passive in may be in the area so that would benefit from your assertiveness. You are never wrong when you ask for what you want. Using a respectful tone and a steady voice ask for what you want. If a person is willing to reach a compromise, you will never know that if you don't ask for the things you need. If you don't stand for yourself, it is unlikely that anyone else will. Make it a priority to advocate for yourself and maintain your boundaries regardless of whether you're at work or in a social situation. Making yourself your own cheerleader can bring you further out of your shell and help you to be a little less shy.

Maintaining your boundaries when you're still trying to get out of your shell and be less timid can be challenging but if you simply use the techniques in this chapter in your daily life, perhaps you can learn to be a bit more assertive. Your assertiveness will not happen overnight but if you consistently make an effort to improve that skill, you can see results within a few weeks. People that had previously taken advantage of the fact that you were not standing firm on where your boundaries are will be surprised to learn that they can no longer push the envelope with you. Learning how to be empathetic to others will help you to also respect their boundaries even when you are being assertive. Now that you know how to assert yourself, it is time to learn the valuable skill of being authentic in everything you do.

Chapter 10:

Embracing Vulnerability

and Authenticity

From an early age society expects you to hide your feelings, especially if they are considered weak. You are told to be brave in the face of adversity and to conquer your fears. This often results in people not wanting to be vulnerable or authentic in how they feel. What is celebrated and glorified are shows of strength and things that seem perfect. Vulnerability and imperfection are often seen as weakness. Your shyness may be exacerbated by your need to cover up your imperfections. When you doubt yourself, it's unlikely that you would want people to see you as you are, which further prohibits you from connecting with others. In this chapter I will teach you how to express how you feel and what you think, without being overcome by the fear of rejection. You will also learn how to be resilient when you feel vulnerable. There is a beauty in being vulnerable and authentically yourself and I will try to highlight it for you in this chapter. Allow those walls to come down and the benefits may surprise you.

Embracing Vulnerability as a Strength in Social Interactions

Vulnerability can mean different things to different people. According to Hussain, "It involves allowing ourselves to be seen, heard, and understood without hiding behind masks or pretenses. It's about acknowledging and accepting our weaknesses, fears, and insecurities, and being willing to share them with others" (2023, para 3). When you are vulnerable you are allowing your emotions to come through and to remain exposed at the risk of experiencing pain or rejection. Vulnerability has the ability to forge stronger and deeper connections with others because it requires you to be your most authentic self. So many of our human interactions take place behind a mask or some kind of façade. When the relationships are based on this inauthentic façade, the connections are weak and fickle. Vulnerability plays a pivotal role in taking your relationships to the next level. Laying yourself bare in front of another human being shows that you trust them, and that you are comfortable enough to be authentic in your truth no matter what that looks like. Vulnerability allows you to open yourself in such a way that it is easier to connect with other people through compassion, empathy, and shared experiences.

In order to truly embrace vulnerability, you have to find a certain courage and strength within yourself. It is normal to feel self-conscious about what you feel and the things you think. Taking the time to reflect on all the times that you shied away from being vulnerable can point to all the different areas where you need to use a little more courage in order to be more vulnerable. In order to have compassion for yourself and accept yourself you need to face yourself as you are. This makes your vulnerability especially hard as you face all your imperfections. Research has shown that vulnerability as displayed by others is often seen as a strength but is viewed as a weakness when looking at it from an internal perspective (Kerr, 2021). A lot of the time you might appreciate vulnerability when it is coming from somebody else rather than when you have to display it yourself. This is because the further you are from a certain situation the less likely you are to see the negative aspects of it. When you are required to display vulnerability, it is very easy to see where the downfalls may occur. Regardless of where the vulnerability is coming from, it is a beautiful thing, and we should always embrace it. Being vulnerable is not a weakness.

Expressing Genuine Emotions and Thoughts to Foster Deeper Connections

Authenticity is a satisfying way of life that you can achieve by understanding who you are and what you want out of life. When you live your life according to your own set of values and principles you are being authentic. There are so many different opinions that may influence what happens in your life: what your parents think, your colleagues' comments or your partner's opinions may have a bearing on the decisions you make in your life. It is not always easy to live authentically, especially if there is pressure from those around you to do things a certain way. When you peel away the mask that you hide behind and show another person your authentic self you are able to reach a mutual understanding with that other person. Furthermore, you will be able to build trust as well as intimacy because your relationship is genuine. When you are able to be authentic in all aspects of your life you experience a greater sense of satisfaction and fulfillment that you are willing to share with others. There is no burden to pretend and keep up appearances; when connecting with others you are more relaxed as there is no need to cover up your tracks. Authenticity allows you to live a life filled with integrity. It is easier to then seek out those who also live an authentic life so that you can forge genuine relationships with them.

Being vulnerable and authentic requires you to step out of your comfort zone a little bit so that you can express how you feel or what you think. This is obviously terrifying because you might wonder if people will judge you or reject how you feel. Fortunately, there is a way that you can overcome your fear of judgment and rejection when you need to express how you truly feel.

- Begin to live with integrity: Allow each and every choice you make to be guided by integrity. No one can make you feel bad about living with integrity.

- Create values that you live by. Find core values that speak to who you are and commit to them. Use them to guide you when you are in ethically challenging situations.

- Always communicate honestly: Speak honestly about your intentions and what you mean while taking the other person's feelings into consideration. Develop emotional intelligence so that you know what is appropriate to say and what is not.

- Avoid making assumptions about what others are thinking.

- Build your self-confidence so that you can stand firm in your truth no matter where you are.

When you stick to living this way, your fear of judgment and rejection will fall away as you stand by your own values. It is much better to stick to what you believe in and remain true to yourself and then try to satisfy other people and their standards. Developing a strong sense of self will help you to overcome the fear of judgment and rejection when expressing how you feel.

To practice open and honest communication, remember to first start by accepting how you feel without paying judgment on yourself. From there you can describe your feelings by labeling them. Take time to listen to how the other person feels as well. Always say 'I feel sad' not 'I am sad'. Accept the other person's feelings in a nonjudgmental way so that they can feel validated and safe. Being vulnerable and allowing others to be vulnerable with you create an authentic environment where deeper connections can thrive.

Overcoming the Fear of Rejection by Being Authentic and True to Oneself

Everyone wants to belong. Very few people want to be on their own and not be a part of a social circle. Something that can hold you back could be your fear of rejection. This could stem from your childhood, where you were either rejected by your caregiver or your peers. The best thing to do is to try to identify where this fear came from. Introspect on your past and try to identify times when you were rejected and how you felt shortly after that. Why did it hurt so much to be rejected and why do you avoid it today? Knowing what your underlying fears and beliefs are that drive you to avoid rejection can bring you a lot closer to being a more authentic version of yourself. Having a strong sense of self-regulation can help you to keep your emotions and behaviors under control even in situations where you are triggered. You can't help but be who you are. Accepting yourself as well as knowing your self-worth can help to shield you against your fear of rejection and judgment. When you are comfortable with who you are and the things you feel and think and then there is hardly anybody who can make you feel bad for that.

You should always remember that at one point or another each and every person on this planet has been rejected. Experiencing rejection does not make you less of a person. Your self-worth should not be tied to the number of times you have been rejected. It's just one of those things that you will have to navigate at least a few times in your life. Develop a thick skin and understand that rejection should not stop you in your tracks and you should keep moving forward with what you want to achieve. Life is filled with so many ups and downs and rejection could be around any corner. Learn to live with rejection and develop resilience in the face of it. It won't matter if people reject what you think or your feelings because you will be at peace with them when you are authentic.

Cultivating Resilience in the Face of Vulnerability and Building Authentic Relationships

There is no guarantee that being vulnerable will always yield positive results. Some people will not respond well to you being your authentic self. In fact, there are some people who dislike it when people are vulnerable. This means that it is essential for your emotional stability to show resilience at the same time you show vulnerability. According to the American Psychological Association, "Psychologists define resilience as the process of adapting well in the face of adversity, trauma, tragedy, threats, or significant sources of stress—such as family and relationship problems, serious health problems, or workplace and financial stressors" (2012, para 4). When other people are not reacting positively to your vulnerability, it is helpful to tell yourself that their reaction is not a defining factor in your life. You should buttress that it is their reaction that is making you feel bad, not the act of being vulnerable itself. There is a chance of rejection every time you reveal who you are. Don't deny feeling pain or distress. Being resilient has nothing to do with pretending everything is ok. Rather, resilience is about coping with life even when things are not alright.

When you are a shy person who is not used to being vulnerable, you may not have a vast social network to rely on for various things. An important support function to have integrated into your life is one or two supportive people who allow you to be vulnerable and authentic in your thoughts and feelings. You will need someone to make you feel safe enough to share and be yourself. Be discerning about who you let into your life. Supportive positive people can enable you to thrive as you stop being shy rather than people who will judge or put you down in your journey. The more your authentic self is appreciated, the more you will want to show it. Keeping the right people around you will ensure that you nurture only authentic relationships based on mutual trust, understanding, and vulnerability.

It took me some time to accept my authentic side and have the courage to show it to those I was getting close to. My shyness perpetuated my fear of judgment and rejection such that I always had a mask on and could not let people know who I really was. After recognizing the power inherent in being vulnerable, I began to use it as my superpower. The connections I make when I am authentically myself are the most profound and fulfilling relationships in my life.

I hope after going through this chapter, you too can find the strength to reveal your true self. It may take a little time and even more effort, but you can learn to be more authentic. It is a gift to be able to express how you feel while having the resilience to face the consequences of being authentic. Unravel yourself and become the person you always wanted to be. You deserve to exist as only one version of yourself, without worrying about anyone else's opinion about what you feel and think. It seems difficult because you didn't think it was possible. Before reading this chapter, you may have had no clue that being vulnerable and authentic was a way of life that you could achieve. Luckily, now you know, and now it is a real possibility. Don't delay any further, give yourself the gift of authenticity today!

Conclusion

For so many years I wasn't able to get out of my own way. It wasn't because I didn't want to stop being shy but because I didn't have the necessary tools to empower myself. My friends and family thought the best way to overcome my shyness was to push me into the deep end of social situations and often when I was triggered by those scenarios, they would comfort me by telling me that I would get over it. My shyness was seen as something that would shrivel away and detach itself from me the older I got. I learned pretty quickly that it was something that would stay with me as an adult for as long as I let it. The problem was that I did not have the necessary guidance and understanding of why I was shy in the first place. That is the same situation you may have found yourself in before you started reading this book. Fortunately for you, I experienced everything similarly and decided that no one else who struggles with being shy had to live their lives that way.

You can now breathe a sigh of relief because you now have a way out of your shyness. You might not have started implementing the techniques in this book, but just knowing that you have them already provides relief and support. Each chapter has given you various qualities to work on. You now have a clearer idea of where to start and how to build your confidence. Before reading this book, you may not have realized that certain triggers and negative thought patterns may keep you in a state of self-doubt. Now you can identify when these triggers come into play and how to stop yourself from getting stuck in negative patterns. A large part of being shy is due to inner dialogue that often perpetuates low self-esteem. I used to struggle with this the most because I would tell myself that I am unable to face my fears and speak to other people confidently. Once I managed to change the way I spoke to myself I also began to gain some courage and belief in myself. With this book, I know that you have now learned empowering self-talk and the kind of affirmations that can help you overcome your shyness.

Your comfort zone is a space that often feels safe and non-threatening, but it is detrimental to personal growth. With the techniques I have provided, you can safely expand the boundaries of your comfort zone and push yourself toward growth and personal satisfaction. Another tool that can help to soothe you and reduce your shyness is mindfulness and being self-aware, which I have thoroughly discussed; these are tools you can use on a daily basis when you are triggered or as you start your day. Being shy can prohibit you from making deep connections with those around you but if you learn the skill of active listening, you can forge more meaningful relationships. Sometimes it is even difficult to face the fact that you suffer from some kind of social anxiety. I know because of this book, you now have the capability to address your social anxiety and the emotional stress you feel because of it. Your shyness may have been affecting your career and your professional relationships but with the strategies I have shared, you are now on your way to new possibilities. With the advancements in technology that allow us to connect with others with minimal human interaction, you might have become even more shy as less social interaction is required of you. I am sure you are going to benefit from the chapter that seeks to improve your socialization skills in today's digital age.

I encourage you to accept your shyness and be authentic with yourself while still remaining assertive and maintaining your boundaries. I recognize that this journey that you have embarked on is not easy. From the first day that you pick up this book to the day that you read this last page, whether you notice it or not, there has been a difference in your life. Whether that difference is a change in mindset or a change in inner dialogue or physical actions that you have taken to overcome your shyness, a small step is still a step. You are a masterpiece in progress, and you should be celebrated as such. If you have been keeping a journal on your progress, take some time to read back to your first few journal entries. Can you believe the person that wrote those entries is the same person as you? It might seem like it is two completely different people. This is because when you follow the advice in this book, you are consistently making efforts to overcome your shyness even when you think not much is happening. When you take *Stop Being Shy* seriously, you deserve to be celebrated every single day for the things that you are pushing yourself to achieve.

Throughout each and every chapter, I am teaching you valuable social skills that will enable you to better communicate with your friends, family, colleagues and even strangers. The social skills will not be perfect on the first try as you have to keep using and perfecting them almost on a daily basis. These are skills that may have seemed terrifying before, such as actively listening and speaking with others. The more you use them the more you attract people into your social circle. Without noticing you are creating numerous opportunities to practice these newfound social skills in a way that will bring you out of your shell and help you to stop being shy. It must be exhilarating for you to use these skills to reach out to others and form connections when you thought this was near impossible. I was always surprised at how other people would respond positively to my new social skills when I had struggled for so long to form connections with other people. You might experience being in this constant state of awe when you notice all the people that gravitate toward you. Once you get started in utilizing all the tips and techniques, I have shared with you, your life will never be the same again.

When you start getting into the groove of things and have gotten comfortable with the various skills you can use to overcome your shyness, I encourage you to keep on pushing the boundaries. When something starts to feel too comfortable, push the boundaries and challenge yourself so that you are not in a stagnant state. Growth is not comfortable, growth is not easy. What is comforting to know is that if I can overcome my shyness then so can you. If I can find a formula that has worked for me then it might likely work for you too. Don't be afraid to customize this book to your liking. You don't have to use it as a copy-and-paste formula but rather you can tweak and adjust it according to what you feel would work for you. Do not be harsh to yourself or rush yourself to make big changes before you are ready. It took me a few months before I could confidently try any techniques that I felt were going to help me to be less timid. The hard work for me was finding what my triggers work and learning how to speak to myself in an uplifting and nurturing way. That might be the easy part for you but expect some bumps along the way. When you get overwhelmed, you can stop and try again tomorrow. There is no need to place extended amounts of pressure on yourself because I know you are doing the best that you can.

If ever you feel like you are not making any progress, then remember that the point is to forge deeper and more meaningful relationships. Use that as your guiding force because soon you will be expanding your social connections and getting to know people you never thought you would. In the end, your life will be so much more meaningful when you overcome your shyness and start to build deeper relationships. If you ever fall off the horse, feel free to start the book all over again to remind yourself why you wanted to stop being shy in the first place. You have the capacity and confidence to be a formidable presence. You are engaging and bright. Other people may not be able to see it but I know you have it in you. Use this book to let that person shine through and to become the best version of yourself.

If this book has made an impact on your life, I would love to hear about it. Remember to kindly leave a review on Amazon and give your honest rating about this book. Your feedback and experience will always be important to me. I am proud of you, and I hope you can go forth into the world with a renewed pride in yourself.

References

23 hilarious shy puns. (n.d.). Punstoppable. https://punstoppable.com/shy-puns

Ahsan, S. (2017, March 27). *Ten famously shy people who proved you can be the strong, silent, successful type.* National Post. https://nationalpost.com/entertainment/celebr ity/ten-famously-shy-people-who-proved-you-can-be-the-strong-silent-successful-type

American Psychological Association. (2012, January 1). *Building your resilience.* American Psychological Association. https://www.apa.org/topics/resilience/buildin g-your-resilience

American Psychological Association. (2017, July). *What is exposure therapy?* American Psychological Association. https://www.apa.org/ptsd-guideline/patients-and-families/exposure-therapy

Assertiveness training. (2023). ACM Training. https://www.acmtraining.co.uk/rtaCourseCont ent/ASSERTIVENESS%20TRAINING%20B OOKLET.doc

Bambora, Z. (n.d.). *What causes overthinking? And how to overcome it.* HopeQure.

https://www.hopequre.com/blogs/what-causes-overthinking-and-how-to-overcome-it

Bigger Futures. (2023, March 30). *Unlocking your potential: A guide to breaking free of your comfort zone.* LinkedIn. https://www.linkedin.com/pulse/unlocking-your-potential-guide-breaking-free-comfort-zone/

Burns, H. (2023, May 9). *How the comfort zone is ruining your life (and how to break free).* New Trader U. https://www.newtraderu.com/2023/05/09/how-the-comfort-zone-is-ruining-your-life-and-how-to-break-free/

Camp, S. (2021, January 9). *Challenging your comfort zone: How to break out the mold and press towards the mark.* Unstoppable Rise. https://www.unstoppablerise.com/the-comfort-zone/

Carducci, B. J. (2017, June). *Everything you ever wanted to know about shyness in an international context: A discussion on shyness and its cultural explanations.* Psychology International. https://www.apa.org/international/pi/2017/06/shyness#

Cherry, K. (2019). *What is behind the psychology of positive thinking?* Verywell Mind. https://www.verywellmind.com/what-is-positive-thinking-2794772

Cross, R., Dillon, K., & Greenberg, D. (2021, January 29). *The secret to building resilience*. Harvard Business Review. https://hbr.org/2021/01/the-secret-to-building-resilience

Cuncic, A. (2022, November 9). *How to practice active listening*. Verywell Mind. https://www.verywellmind.com/what-is-active-listening-3024343

Department of Health & Human Services. (2015). *Breathing to reduce stress*. Better Health. https://www.betterhealth.vic.gov.au/health/healthyliving/breathing-to-reduce-stress

Ekua, D., & Quansah, E. (2016). *Effect of shyness on peer interaction: A systematic literature review*. In Jönköping University. https://www.diva-portal.org/smash/get/diva2:934436/FULLTEXT01.pdf

Foynes, M. (2021, July 1). *Cultivating self-compassion to counteract self-criticism*. Melissa Foynes. https://melissafoynes.com/cultivating-self-compassion/

Frank, J. L., Reibel, D., Broderick, P., Cantrell, T., & Metz, S. (2013). Mindfulness in education: An approach to cultivating self-awareness that can bolster kids' learning. *Mindfulness*, *6*(2), 208–216. https://doi.org/10.1007/s12671-013-0246-2

Fritscher, L. (2019). *How to overcome a fear of rejection*. Verywell Mind.

https://www.verywellmind.com/what-is-the-fear-of-rejection-2671841

Hailey, L. (2022, April 12). *How not to be shy: 6 strategies for confidently socializing.* Science of People. https://www.scienceofpeople.com/how-not-to-be-shy/

Heggem, M. (2019, November 15). *How to create a safe space for communication with your employees.* Linkedin. https://www.linkedin.com/pulse/how-create-safe-space-communication-your-employees-mathew-heggem/

How do you use open-ended questions to encourage active listening and dialogue? (n.d.). LinkedIn. https://www.linkedin.com/advice/0/how-do-you-use-open-ended-questions-encourage

Hussain, R. (2023, April 11). *Unveiling the beauty of authenticity: Embracing vulnerability in life's journey.* Sports Keeda. https://www.sportskeeda.com/health-and-fitness/embracing-vulnerability-the-courage-show-up-authentically-life

Jenkins, P. (2023, April 7). *The importance of listening: Unlocking the power of effective communication.* Brilliantio. https://brilliantio.com/importance-of-listening/

JMAZ. (2022, June 4). *21 signs you have poor personal boundaries.* Mazzastick.

https://www.mazzastick.com/poor-personal-boundaries/

Kerr, N. (2021, October 28). *The Benefits of Letting Yourself Be Vulnerable.* Psychology Today. https://www.psychologytoday.com/us/blog/social-influence/202110/the-benefits-letting-yourself-be-vulnerable

Lamothe, C. (2019, November 15). *How to stop overthinking: 14 strategies.* Healthline. https://www.healthline.com/health/how-to-stop-overthinking

Martins, J. (2023, January 9). *6 tips to build rapport and develop meaningful relationships.* Asana. https://asana.com/resources/building-rapport

Mayo Clinic Staff. (2020, May 29). *Stressed out? Be assertive.* Mayo Clinic. https://www.mayoclinic.org/healthy-lifestyle/stress-management/in-depth/assertive/art-20044644

Mayo Clinic Staff. (2022, February 3). *Positive thinking: Stop negative self-talk to reduce stress.* Mayo Clinic. https://www.mayoclinic.org/healthy-lifestyle/stress-management/in-depth/positive-thinking/art-20043950

Merriam-Webster Dictionary. (n.d.). *Definition of shy.* Merriam-Webster. https://www.merriam-webster.com/dictionary/shy?utm_campaign=sd&utm_medium=serp&utm_source=jsonld

Mikhail, A. (2022, October 6). *Self-affirmations can boost your confidence and reduce stress.* Fortune Well. https://fortune.com/well/2022/10/06/self-affirmations-can-improve-your-confidence-heres-how-to-start/

Miller, C. (2021, July 12). *6 mindfulness strategies to reduce your overthinking.* Carla Miller Training. https://www.carlamillertraining.com/blog/reducing-overthinking

Mind Tools Content Team. (n.d.). *Authenticity.* MindTools. https://www.mindtools.com/ay30irc/authenticity

Morin, D. A., & Watkins, N. (2022, January 6). *How to be more present and mindful in conversations.* Social Self. https://socialself.com/blog/be-present-conversations/

National Institute of Mental Health. (2022). *Social anxiety disorder: More than just shyness.* National Institute of Mental Health. https://www.nimh.nih.gov/health/publications/social-anxiety-disorder-more-than-just-shyness

OECD. (2019). *How's life in the digital age?: Opportunities and risks of the digital transformation for people's well-being.* OECD Publishing. https://www.oecd.org/publications/how-s-life-in-the-digital-age-9789264311800-en.htm

Page, O. (2020, November 4). *How to leave your comfort zone and enter your "growth zone."* Positive

Psychology. https://positivepsychology.com/comfort-zone/

Plata, M. (2018, October 31). *How to spot your emotional triggers.* Psychology Today. https://www.psychologytoday.com/us/blog/the-gen-y-psy/201810/how-spot-your-emotional-triggers

Platero, A. (2021, February 26). *Identifying your triggers.* Psychology Today. https://www.psychologytoday.com/us/blog/reflect-and-reset/202102/identifying-your-triggers

Prossack, A. (2022, February 28). *5 ways to step outside of your comfort zone.* Forbes. https://www.forbes.com/sites/ashiraprossack1/2022/02/28/5-ways-to-step-outside-of-your-comfort-zone/?sh=15d819e56ed8

Psychology Today Staff. (2019). *Shyness.* Psychology Today. https://www.psychologytoday.com/us/basics/shyness

RAIN: Mindfulness technique (worksheet). (n.d.). Therapist Aid. https://www.therapistaid.com/therapy-worksheet/rain-mindfulness-technique

Raypole, C. (2020a, May 28). *Visualization meditation: 5 exercises to try.* Healthline. https://www.healthline.com/health/visualization-meditation

Raypole, C. (2020b, August 20). *Assertive communication is healthy, not "bossy" — here's why.* Healthline. https://www.healthline.com/health/assertive-communication

Reid, S. (2023, March 22). *Empathy.* Help Guide. https://www.helpguide.org/articles/relationships-communication/empathy.htm

Sanok, J. (2022, April 14). *A guide to setting better boundaries.* Harvard Business Review. https://hbr.org/2022/04/a-guide-to-setting-better-boundaries

Scott, E. (2019). *Positive self talk for a better life.* Verywell Mind. https://www.verywellmind.com/how-to-use-positive-self-talk-for-stress-relief-3144816

Self doubt and overthinking. (2022, June 7). The Inner Challenge. https://30dayschallenge.org/personal-growth/self-doubt-and-overthinking/

Self esteem and assertiveness. (n.d.). Stop It Now. https://www.stopitnow.org.uk/concerned-about-your-own-thoughts-or-behaviour/concerned-about-use-of-the-internet/self-help/moving-forward/self-esteem-and-assertiveness/

Smith, M., & Segal, J. (2019, June 3). *Social anxiety disorder.* HelpGuide. https://www.helpguide.org/articles/anxiety/social-anxiety-disorder.htm

Stritof, S. (2023, January 17). *How to express your feelings.* Verywell Mind. https://www.verywellmind.com/share-your-feelings-with-your-spouse-2300518

Sutton, J. (2022a, January 28). *How to use mindfulness therapy for anxiety: 15 exercises.* Positive Psychology. https://positivepsychology.com/mindfulness-for-anxiety/

Sutton, J. (2022b, February 12). *Visualization in therapy: 16 simple techniques & tools.* Positive Psychology. https://positivepsychology.com/visualization-techniques/

Vilhauer, J. (2020, December 31). *How to create positive affirmations that really work.* Psychology Today. https://www.psychologytoday.com/intl/blog/living-forward/202012/how-create-positive-affirmations-really-work

What are visualization techniques? (n.d.). Self Pause. https://selfpause.com/visualization/what-are-visualization-techniques/

Made in the USA
Las Vegas, NV
01 March 2024

86540776R00075